Rivoli

Beadwork

By Jean Power

Rivoli Beadwork is written and published by Jean Power
www.jeanpower.com / Copyright © 2018 Jean Power
ISBN 10 - 0-9574568-3-2
ISBN 13 - 9780957456839

First Edition - published November 2018

I love to support and encourage any individuals who make
beadwork and sell or gift what they make. Please feel free to
use anything you make from instructions in this book as gifts
or to sell to support your bead buying habit!
However, this right only extends to individuals and also
doesn't extend to teaching the work or copying the
instructions.

Printed by CreateSpace

There are many people I would like to thank who have helped
this book to come to fruition:
- All the lovely ladies I have named projects after (whether
  within these pages or elsewhere). I love having you in my
  life and am so lucky to do so
- Caroline Keen who kindly proofread everything for me
  and offers me lots of help & guidance
- My one-man support band who cheers me on no matter
  what I do and always lets me know that he's behind me
  100%. You keep me sane when I'm working 18 hour
  days and talk me down from the ceiling when I'm getting
  in a fizz taking photos. Without you none of this would
  ever have been possible. Thank you

Please note that I have tried my best to ensure that these
instructions are accurate but if you spot any errors, have any
queries, or would like to show me photos of anything you
have done from the book (and I would love to see them!)
please contact me through my website at:

www.jeanpower.com

where you can also find any future corrections or additions to
the book, buy patterns & kits, discover classes or sign-up to
my newsletter

Welcome

When I first began beading I kept it simple and stuck with seed beads and geometric beading...

...But one day I added some crystals to my work... and immediately realised how foolish I'd been in not doing that before!

Then, just over a decade ago, I discovered crystal Rivolis and I've not looked back since. These little circles of sparkle add so much colour & light to beadwork that I can't resist using them as much as possible and over time I have bezelled literally thousands of them. So, it only seemed natural to gather some of my favourite designs into a book and take the time to develop other new ones to accompany them.

My desire for this book is to give you lots of projects & ideas so that you too can grow your love of Rivolis and create the crystal beadwork you love and want to wear.

I have included beaded projects made with a wide range of beads and encompassing a plethora of styles, shapes, sizes and difficulty levels.

I have also tried to take many of the projects, techniques & ideas on a journey so each one has at least one variation or option you can bead instead. There are also many others scattered throughout, for example have a look at **Bicone Snowflakes** for a project that can be stopped at any of Steps 2,3,4,5, or 6, to give you a completely different outcome.

The same is true of many of the other projects and I hope you find that altering a bead here, or a step there, will give you your own unique, sparkling beadwork to be proud of.

So, whether you want something subtle, or to dazzle people all around, dive right in and happy beading!

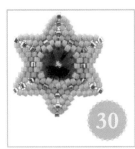

Basics

158

Seed Beads

72

164

Pearls

102

Geometric

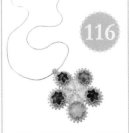

116

Extra Sparkle

128

166

Shaped Beads

154

Basics

Get started with all the basics
essential for the sparkling
projects in this book...

Materials

The first place to start with all of the projects within these pages is with the right materials...

Seed & Cylinder beads

These are the basis of all beadwork and are used throughout this book to accompany and create bezels for the Rivolis.

Seed beads and cylinder beads differ in their shape with seed beads resembling ring doughnuts and cylinder beads being small sections of a tube (or cylinder, hence the name).

Cylinder bead is the generic term for the style of bead. Some examples of brand names they're sold under are Delicas, Aikos and Treasures.

Both of these beads are numbered for their sizes and the higher the number the smaller the bead

Seed beads are more rounded which makes them perfect for adding a softer look and texture to your beadwork

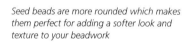

Cylinder beads have flat sides which make them ideal for geometric beadwork

> **TOP TIP**
> DB on the 'I Used' section of a project means 'Delica Bead' and is telling you exactly what colour I used

> **TOP TIP**
> All Rivoli and pearl colours given are Swarovski unless stated otherwise

Thread

There is a huge amount that can be written about beading threads and, like everyone, I have my own preferences which I generally stick to, only changing when it's necessary for a project.

My main advice when it comes to choosing thread is simple: use what YOU love.

I prefer a more flexible thread with a stretch such a Miyuki, Nymo, One G, KO etc. as I find that the lack of stretch in Fireline makes it harder for me to manipulate my work in the way that I want. But I know many beaders for whom the exact opposite is true.
However, when I'm using Swarovski Pearls or bicones with sharp edges, and know my thread may be cut by them, I switch to Fireline for extra security.
So experiment and see what works best for you and the project you're beading

Shaped Beads

Shaped beads are great for adding extra texture and shape detail to your Rivoli beadwork and this book uses both SuperDuos and Crescents for this

> **TOP TIP**
> *When beading with any 2-hole beads always check both holes before using them as often the coating can block one of the holes and it's very annoying if you don't spot it until it's beaded into your work…*

Rivoli Alternatives

Why not use buttons or other 14mm cabochons in place of Rivolis?

You may need to adjust the project you're beading for the depth of the focal you're using, but do experiment as you can get amazing results….

Manufacturers & Brand Names

There are many bead manufacturers in the world but for the precise beadwork that bezelling Rivolis usually entails you'll want to use precision beads and so I recommend a few manufacturers for different items:

You may find Rivolis that are made by Swarovski (as shown on the left above) have much finer edges and facets compared to those made by other manufacturers (as can be seen on the right in the photo)

- **Rivolis**
  Most of this book is done using Swarovski Rivolis and the colour names I quote are theirs or 'aftermarket coatings' added to Swarovski stones. These are accurately sized, incredibly sparkly and come in a wide variety of colours & finishes. You can also get Rivolis made in the Czech Republic or China but be aware that these may be deeper and less precise so any projects you bead may need to be adjusted to allow for this

- **Seed beads**
  I prefer Miyuki seed beads which are made in Japan as their smaller, more rounded, 'more doughnut like' shape is perfect for bezelling and beading all of the projects in this book

- **Cylinder beads**
  Throughout the book I have used Miyuki Delica beads, but do experiment with other brands

- **Pearls & Bicones**
  All the pearls and bicones I use in the book are made by Swarovski, but again do experiment with other brands and other types & sizes of beads just keeping an eye out for whether any size or shape differences mean you need to adjust the project

Tips, Techniques & Terminology

All the basic guidance essential to help you with bezelling Rivolis...

Circle Through

This means to thread through a bead (or beads) in the same direction that you previously went through it

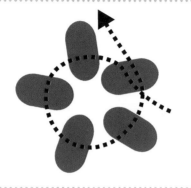

Back Through/ Thread Back Through

This means to thread through a bead (or beads) in the opposite direction than you previously went through it

Read Through

I really recommend reading through each project before you begin as they all contain lots of extra tips & variations which give you advice & options that you won't want to miss.

I also very strongly recommend that you read through every step before you attempt it as the entire text has all the information you need and you may miss something vital if you leap in before fully reading or understanding what you need to do

The Diagrams

All the diagrams in this book follow the same format:

- All coloured beads are those being added in that step
- All grey beads are those previously added
- The bead with a dot on it is the first one you'll add in the step
- The thread is sometimes shown on top of your beads. This is just for clarity and when this is done the thread will be 'dotted'
- Often the diagrams will show more space than will be in your actual beadwork but this is just so you can see what is happening and in reality you don't want extra space between your beads

Row vs. Round

- Rows are where you weave back and forth from one side to another. For example these are used in **Beaded Tabs** (see Page 20)

- Rounds are where you bead around in a circle and the beginning and end are right next to each other (most of the projects in this book use rounds)

Impact

When you bead anything, all that you do has an impact on what has been beaded before, even work many rows or rounds back.
This is especially true when decreasing as it can take a few rounds of further beadwork to pull those first few rounds into place.
So stick with it; every bit of extra beading you do adds extra thread, extra substance, extra decoration, extra security and extra shaping, all of which have an impact on the end result

Bold Text In The Instructions

Whenever you see bold text (**such as this**) in any project instructions its referring you to a technique or project elsewhere within the book. You can either find out where on the Contents Page, under 'Techniques' or by the Page number given

Stitch-In-The-Ditch

Stitch-In-The-Ditch (referred to as SITD in the book) is when you bead on top of some already done beadwork (usually Peyote Stitch) adding in new beads which sit in the spaces 'or ditches' between the beads.

Most of the time this is referred to in the projects you'll be doing it on top of the central round of C beads on a bezel made using the **Basic Bezelling Technique**

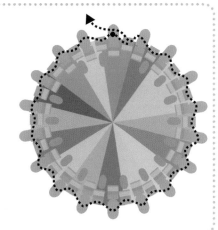

Abbreviations

- **B -** This indicates a bicone crystal (whatever size is in your materials list)
- **B3 -** This stands for a 3mm bicone crystal
- **B4 -** Indicates a 4mm bicone crystal
- **C -** This stands for cylinder bead
- **CR -** This means a Crescent Bead
- **DB -** This means Delica Bead and refers to the colour number of the bead I used in a project
- **P -** Stands for Pearl
- **RAW -** This abbreviation stands for 'Right-Angle-Weave'
- **SD -** Stands for SuperDuo
- **SITD -** This abbreviation is short for 'Stitch-In-The-Ditch'
- **S8 -** Lets you know when to use a size 8 seed bead
- **S11 -** Indicates a size 11 seed bead
- **S15 -** Refers to size 15 seed bead

Look at your work

This really is my top tip for all beading!

As you work look carefully at what you're creating. This is how you'll learn what effect the different things you do will have and where you can spot if something is going wrong (or right!) and it will save you the annoyance of having to later undo your work if an error slips past you

Experiment

'I wonder what will happen if I...' is the best question you can ask yourself as you bead.
Every single project in this book grew out of that question and me then taking the time to experiment with the idea
Each project in this book also has many possible variations that can grow out of making small changes to any of the steps in its instructions

Repeat From * to *

Any time you see this in the instructions you're being asked to repeat what was written previously between the asterisks as many times as you're told to.
An example is:

*Pick up 1 x C and thread into the next space, bead a **Peyote Stitch Decrease** in the next space*. Repeat from * to * five more times.

So you would end up adding 6 single beads, each one followed by a **Peyote Stitch Decrease** (see below)

Knots

I don't tie a knot when I begin my work as it can hold the work too tight and fill the bead holes.
The only time I make an exception to this is when beading **Distorted Squares** as then I want the work to be held very tightly

Variations

I have given you lots of ideas for variations with every project but do dive in and see what other ones you can come up with...

Peyote Stitch Decrease

These are beaded using the same thread-path as you would bead regular Peyote Stitch but with no bead on your thread

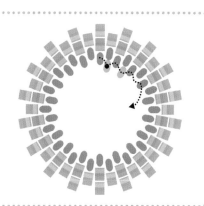

Basic Bezelling Technique - 14mm Rivoli

Bezelling a Rivoli is the act of surrounding or encasing the Rivoli. In this book that means using beads and beadwork to secure, decorate and adorn a Rivoli so it can be used either by itself, or with others, to create a piece of jewellery

A Bezel

A bezel needs to be strong and secure so that your Rivoli doesn't fall out but it also needs to be attractive and allow the Rivoli to shine out - combining the two elements can be a real challenge sometimes!

This book uses a mixture of different beads, stitches and techniques to make bezels but a lot of the designs use the Basic Bezelling Technique described here.

THE BASIC BEZEL

STEP 1
Rounds 1-2.
On your thread pick up 36 x C beads and circle through the first 2 to join into a ring (36 x C).

> **TOP TIP**
> *Circling through 2 beads in Step 1 leaves your thread tail in the right place to continue in Step 5.*

STEP 2
Round 3.
Using C beads and Peyote Stitch add 1 round with 1 bead in every space. Pull tight so that the beads don't have spaces between them (18 x C).

> **TOP TIP**
> *At the end of every round you will Step-Up to exit the first bead added in that round to be ready to continue*

> **TOP TIP**
> *If bezelling a Rivoli which is deeper than a Swarovski then, after Step 2, you may need to add another 1-2 rounds of C beads just as you did in Step 2*

> **TOP TIP**
> *In Steps 3-4 you switch to smaller beads (S15s) and move on from beading a straight-sided piece of beadwork to wanting your new rounds to pull in and make the opening in your beadwork smaller. It is the combination of smaller beads and pulling your thread tight, which will hold your Rivoli safe*

> **TOP TIP**
> *If you know you want to add a **Star Design** to your work (Page 16) then I recommend adding it after Step 4 when it's easiest to bead*

STEP 3
Round 4.
Using S15 beads and Peyote Stitch add 1 round with 1 bead in every space (18 x S15).

STEP 4
Round 5.
Repeat Step 3 to add another round of S15 beads making sure to pull tight to reduce the opening in your beadwork (18 x S15).

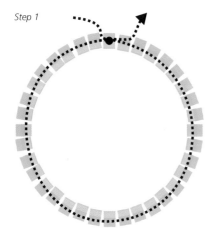

Step 1

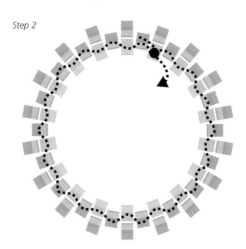

Step 2

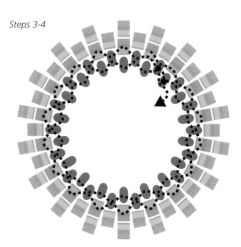

Steps 3-4

TOP TIP

For Step 5 the beads you need to locate in Round 1 can be distinguished as they stick out further from the S15 beads than the others, also your thread tail will be coming out of one of them. There will be 18 of them and you can begin the next step exiting any of them

TOP TIP

If you want to fully cover the back of your Rivoli then read on. But, if you don't want to fully cover the back, but need to add some extra security to your bezel, then see **Securing The Back - Optional** *on the next page*

Step 5
Either return to your tail thread or weave your working thread to exit any C bead in Round 1 of your work.

STEP 6
Round 6.
Repeat Step 3 to add a round of S15 beads here at what will be the back of your work (18 x S15).

STEP 7
Insert your Rivoli so that it faces out from the S15 beads added in Steps 3-4.

STEP 8
Round 7.
Add another round of S15 beads making sure to pull tight so that your Rivoli is held securely in place (18 x S15).

COVERING THE BACK
This is optional but gives a nice finish to your work and preserves any coating there is on the back of the Rivoli. You may find you need to adjust what you bead depending on your Rivoli and seed beads.

STEP 9
*Add 1 x S15 into each of the next 2 spaces and then bead a **Peyote Stitch Decrease** (Page 11) in the third*. Repeat from * to * five more times and then Step-Up to exit the first bead added (12 x S15).

STEP 10
Add a round with 1 x S15 in each space including the larger spaces where you decreased in the previous step (12 x S15)..

STEP 11
*Add 1 x S15 into each of the next 2 spaces and then bead a **Peyote Stitch Decrease** in the third*. Repeat from * to * three more times and then Step-Up to exit the first bead added (8 x S15 – green in the diagram).

STEP 12
Add a round with 1 x S15 in each space including the larger spaces where you decreased in the previous step (8 x S15 – orange in the diagram.

STEP 13
*Add 1 x S15 into a space and then bead a **Peyote Stitch Decrease** in the next space*. Repeat from * to * three more times and then Step-Up to exit the first bead added (4 x S15 – blue in the diagram).

STEP 14
Add a round with 1 x S15 in each space including the larger spaces where you decreased in the previous step (4 x S15 – yellow in the diagram).

STEP 15
Weave all around the 4 beads added in the last step to bring them together.

TOP TIP

The diagram for Steps 6-8 shows your new rounds as coming out further from your work but in reality you'll be pulling tight and they will be coming into the centre of your work as in this diagram

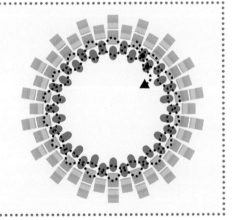

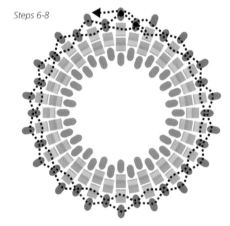

Steps 6-8

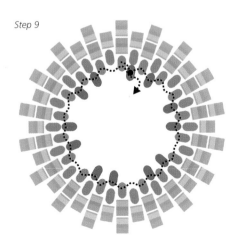

Step 9

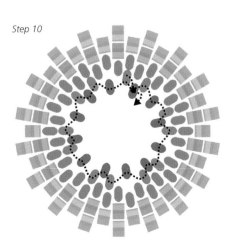

Step 10

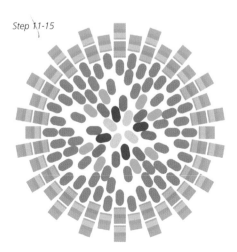

Step 11-15

Securing The Back- Optional

If you don't want to completely cover the back of your Rivoli, but you feel your bezel needs some extra security, you have a few different options:

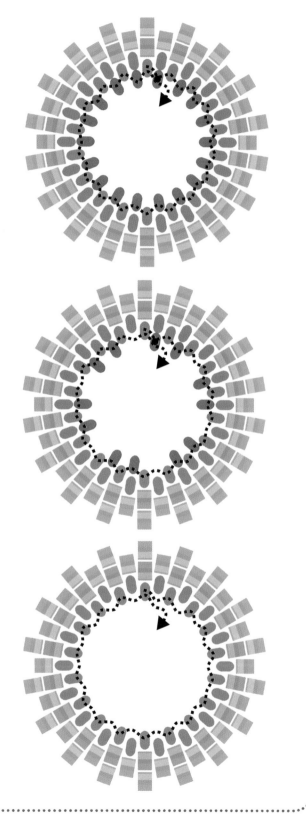

- You can add another round of S15 beads (or smaller seed beads or Charlottes (a very small seed bead) if you need something smaller) making sure to pull tight

- You can also bead a decreasing round using **Peyote Stitch Decreases** (Page 11) by adding 1 x S15 into each of the next 2 spaces and then threading through the next as though beading Peyote Stitch but with no bead on your thread. Make sure to pull tight

- You can weave all through the S15 beads in the last round added, with no new beads on your thread, pulling tight

Bezelling Other Sizes of Rivolis

Bezelling all the other common sizes of Rivolis is based on exactly the same method as described for a 14mm Rivoli (Page 12) – the only difference is the number of beads you pick up in the first step and therefore how many beads will be in each round as you continue:

THE BASIC BEZEL

STEP 1

Rounds 1-2. On your thread pick up as many C beads as needed for the size Rivoli you're bezelling and circle through the first 2 to join into a ring.

STEP 2

Round 3. Using C beads and Peyote Stitch add 1 round with 1 bead in every space. Pull tight so that the beads don't have spaces between them.

STEP 3

Rounds 4-5. Using S15 beads and Peyote Stitch add 2 rounds with 1 bead in every space.

STEP 4

Either return to your tail thread or weave your working thread to exit any C bead in Round 1 of your work.

STEP 5

Round 6. Repeat the principle of Step 3 to add a round of S15 beads here at what will be the back of your work.

STEP 7

Insert your Rivoli so that it faces out from the S15 beads added in Step 3.

STEP 8

Round 7. Add another round of S15 beads making sure to pull tight so that your Rivoli is held securely in place.

> **TOP TIP**
> All of the projects in this book can potentially be adapted for the different sizes of Rivolis (especially those based on the Basic Bezelling technique) so do dive in and experiment…

> **TOP TIP**
> You can add a **Star Design** to a 12 or 16mm Rivoli bezelled as described, or a 18mm Rivoli if you use 48 beads as described in the Tip elsewhere on this page

10mm
- 26 C beads for Step 1
- 13 beads in each round

12mm
- 30 C beads for Step 1
- 15 beads in each round

16mm
- 42 C beads for Step 1
- 21 beads in each round

18mm
- 46 C beads for Step 1
- 23 beads in each round

> **TOP TIP**
> You may have success using just 40, or 44, beads at Step 1 for your 16mm Rivoli which will give you 20, or 22, beads per round but you won't be able to add a **Star Design**

> **TOP TIP**
> You may have success using 48 beads at Step 1 for your 18mm Rivoli which will give you 24 beads per round and means you can add a **Star Design** to the front

Adding Star Designs

A Star design can be added to any 12 or 14mm Rivoli project which uses the Basic Bezelling Technique (see Pages 12-14) and adds some extra decoration and pizazz to your work using just 15-18 seed beads!

TOP TIP

*Adding the Star Design when beading your bezel is completely optional. It is easiest to add it after Step 4 in the **Basic Bezelling Technique** but you can add a new thread to your work and bead the Star at any time after that if desired*

ADDING A STAR DESIGN TO A 14MM RIVOLI

STEP 1

Weave to exit any S15 bead in the last round of S15 beads added at the start of your work.

Step 1

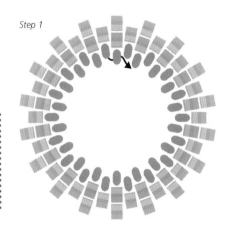

TOP TIP

Weaving through beads in previous rounds in the next steps ensures you don't have threads showing where you have spaces with no beads added in

STEP 2

Round 1.

Using S15 beads and Peyote Stitch *add 1 bead into each of the next 2 spaces.

You want to leave the next space empty and so need to weave down (carrying on moving in the same direction you already were) 1 x S15 bead in Round 4 on your bezel and then up the next S15 bead in Round 5 on your bezel.*

Repeat from * to * five more times to add 10 more S15 beads to your round, making sure to Step-Up at the end of the round to exit the first S15 bead added (12 x S15).

STEP 3

Round 2.

You're now going to bead a round with S15 beads just in the spaces between where you added S15 beads in the previous round.

Peyote stitch 1 x S15 bead into the next space. Then thread diagonally down 2 x S15 beads and then up 2 x S15 beads in previous rounds to bring you to the next space between S15 beads added in the previous round.

Repeat from * to * 5 more times to add a total of 6 x S15 beads/ Points to the round to finish (6 x S15).

Step 2

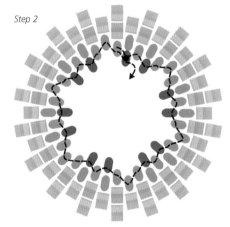

Step 3

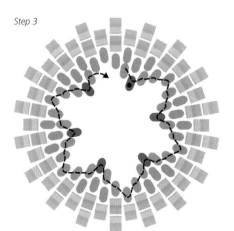

PLACEMENT

If adding the Star Design before you do any further beading on your Rivoli then you can exit any S15 bead as it doesn't matter where the Star Points lie.

But, if you are adding your Star Design after you have finished your Rivoli beadwork, then you may want to plan out where the Points of the Star sit and so make sure you exit the S bead 2 beads to the left or right of where you want the Star Point to sit (2 to the left if you're beading clockwise and 2 to the right if you're beading anticlockwise)

ADDING A STAR DESIGN TO A 12MM RIVOLI

This is beaded using exactly the same principle as **Adding a Star Design** to a 14mm Rivoli, but picking up a different number of beads in each step:

- Step 2 – you'll bead this just 5 times in total using 10 x S15
- Step 3 – uses 5 x S15

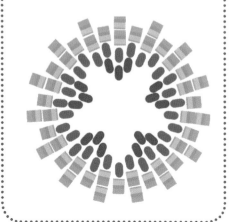

Isotoxal Stars

Varying the principle of adding a Star Design gives you a whole new world of ornamentation

TOP TIP

Make sure to read the tip on placement on the previous page before you begin

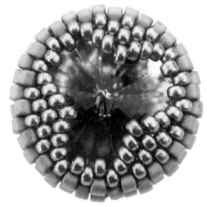

ADDING AN ISOTOXAL STAR DESIGN TO A 14MM RIVOLI
STEP 1
Weave to exit any S15 bead on the last round of S15 beads at the front of your bezel.

TOP TIP

Weaving through beads in previous rounds in the next steps ensures you don't have threads showing in the spaces with no beads added in

STEP 2
Round 1.
Using S15 beads and Peyote Stitch add 1 bead into each of the next 3 spaces. You want to leave the next 3 spaces empty and so need to weave (carrying on moving in the same direction as you already were) through the 2 previous S15 rounds until you are in the 4th space along.
Repeat from * to * 2 more times to add a total of 9 x S15 beads in the round.
Make sure you Step-Up at the end of the round to exit the first S15 bead added (9 x S15).

STEP 3
Round 2.
Add 1 x S15 bead into each of the 2 spaces between S15 beads added in the last round. Just as you did in Step 2 weave through previously added beads to bring you to the next space between S15 beads added in the last round.
Continue adding S15 beads just between the S15 beads added in the last round until you have added 6 in total (6 x S15).

STEP 4
Round 3.
Add 1 x S15 bead into just the spaces between S15 beads added in the last round. Just as you did in Step 2 weave through previously added beads to bring you to the next space between S15 beads added in the last round.
Continue adding S15 beads just between the S15 beads added in the last round until you have added 3 in total (3 x S15).

Step 2

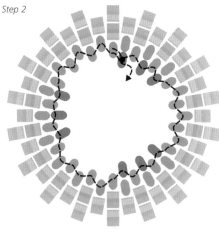

Step 3

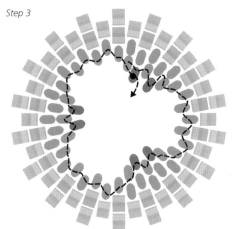

Step 4

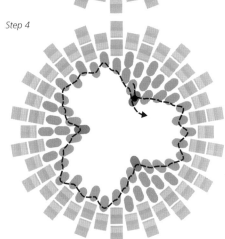

VARIATION

To bead the variation shown here in Round 1 you can also add 1 x S15 bead in the central space of the 3 spaces where you miss adding beads in the original version

Playing With Bezels

All the projects, techniques and ideas in this book can be mixed-and-matched with each other in many different ways and here are some to get you inspired...

Earrings

All of the Rivoli bezels in this book can be made into earrings in a variety of different ways. You can look at the earring projects already included for instructions but here are some ideas to get you started:

- Earring finding threaded through a bead (as I did with my **Susie Qs**)

- Loop of seed beads (see **Bicone Snowflakes** for an example of this)

- Earring finding stitched into the beadwork (see **Crystal Coronas** for an example of this)

- A beaded Triangle with an earring post beaded into it (see **Mixed Shape Set** to see this in action)

Earring findings can be threaded straight through larger seed beads in your bezel

Your bezel can be turned into an earring with a loop of seed beads attaching an earring finding

Beaded Bails

There are 3 Bails I have used for projects in this book; A Full Distorted Square (**Mixed Shapes Set**); a Distorted Square with an empty centre (**Flying Vs**); and a beaded triangle (**Mixed Shapes Set**).
Any of these, or the principles of them, can be added to any of the other projects to turn them into pendant or earrings.

You could also use other bezels as bails. For example a **Triangle Bezel** would be perfect to hang a **Layered Triangle Pendant** from

Hanging Loops

Hanging loops are simple strands of beads which can be added to the back, or edge, of your work to hang your piece from. Their addition means your bezel can be used as a pendant or earrings or even a brooch

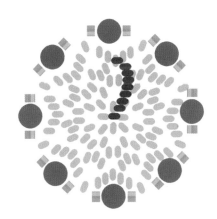

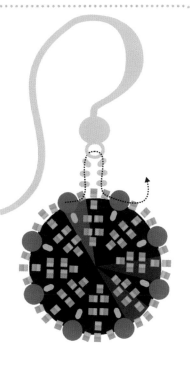

Tassels & Drops

These can be simply added to edges of your bezels either by using loops of seed beads, jump rings or by stitching them into your beadwork (see **Claw Bezels** for an example).

If you use tassels you can also add extra decoration by adding beaded covers to them

Quick & Easy Brooch

You can turn any bezel with a hanging loop at the back into a brooch by simply using a safety pin (which is hidden inside your clothes):

From the inside of your clothes, or coat, thread your safety pin to the outside, loop under the beaded loop with the safety pin and then thread back into your clothes and do up the safety pin to finish

Rivoli Medals

One of my favourite things to do with a bezelled Rivoli is... replicate it!

My Rivoli Medals necklace is made up of Rivolis bezelled using the **Basic Bezelling Technique** and then each has a **Beaded Tab** (see the next page) added which is 4 beads wide and 15 rows long (each end begins or is zipped to an outside round of C beads on the bezel).

As these mix-and-match bezels are designed to be strung on a metal neck wire, I then made 30 beaded beads (I began by picking up 8 C beads and then added 16 more rows for a total of 18 before zipping the edges together).

Having this many beaded beads means that I can string my Medals in lots of different combinations (some of which are shown here).

This necklace technique can be adapted to any of the bezels in the book which use the **Basic Bezelling Technique** – you just may need to adjust the Hanging Tab or beaded beads to ensure everything fits together

Beaded Tabs

Lots of the project instructions in this book include Tabs to hang the bezel from. But, even if the instructions don't specify Tabs, all of the bezels in this book can have them and they can be added to your bezel in a variety of different ways. Here are the basic techniques I use:

PEYOTE STITCH

Begin by choosing where you want the tab to sit plus how wide you want it to be, and therefore where you'll begin exiting your beadwork (you'll exit a bead before the space where you want to add your first bead at the edge of the tab)

• Even-Count Peyote Stitch Tab

STEP 1 - Begin beading using Peyote Stitch and the beads of your choice until you have made it as wide as desired.

Step 1 - Even-Count Peyote Stitch

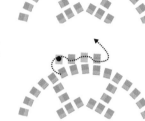

STEP 2 - Then simply turn to bead another row.

STEP 3 - Once it is as long as you want, fold the tab over and zip the end to your bezel.

Step 2 - Even-Count Peyote Stitch

• Odd-Count Peyote Stitch Tab

STEP 1 - Begin beading using Peyote Stitch and the beads of your choice until you have made it as wide as desired.

Step 1 - Odd-Count Peyote Stitch

STEP 2 - Weave through your work to exit the last bead added and then bead another row.

Step 2 - Odd-Count Peyote Stitch

> **TOP TIP**
> *Changing direction to exit the last bead added is much easier when you have more beadwork to thread through, but when there isn't much, such as in the **Crystal Cage** being shown, then you may have to weave a little distance away and then work your way back, or you can use the turning method described under **Rivoli Triangle Heart** or **Star Flowers***

> **TOP TIP**
> *Exactly what you do with Odd-Count Peyote Stitch can vary as to how wide your Tab is*

STEP 3 - Once it is as long as you want, fold the tab over and zip the end to your bezel.

LADDER STITCH

You can simply stitch single beads onto a bead at the edge of your bezel (it doesn't have to be at a corner) using Ladder Stitch and then join the last one back to your bezel again. This means you can hang single bezels (such as the **Crystal Cage** shown here) as an earring or pendant.

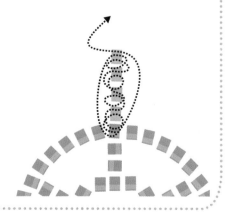

Tabs for Joining

Tabs, as described under **Beaded Tabs** on the previous page, can also be used to join different bezels. Simply begin a tab on one bezel and then, when it's as long as you want or need, zip it to the other bezel.

This is what I used here in this simple bezelled buttons bracelet in which each 14mm button was bezelled using the **Basic Bezelling Technique**

All Kinds of Rings

Beaded Tabs (of any kind - see previous page) can be varied so that they begin at one side of your bezel and then join to the other side which gives you a loop which means your bezel can now be a finger ring or scarf ring. All of the bezels in this book can have this done to them...

Tabs for Linking

You can also use **Beaded Tabs** (see previous page) added to opposite edges of bezels to link them together. For example, I could have added tabs to my **Pearl Buds** and linked them to the beaded Links with those rather than the loops of seed beads I did use

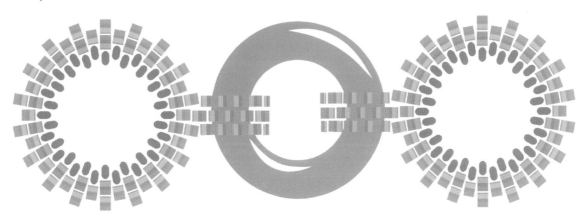

You can also link tabs like this with large jump rings or simple loops of beads

Joining with RAW

Different bezels can also be joined together using Right-Angle-Weave (RAW). You can add as many or as few units as you need, or like the look of

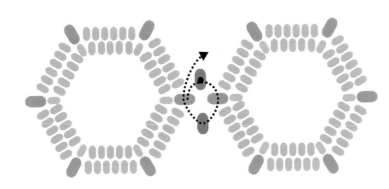

Seed Beads

Learn how to create beautiful
Rivoli-based beadwork using
just seed beads...

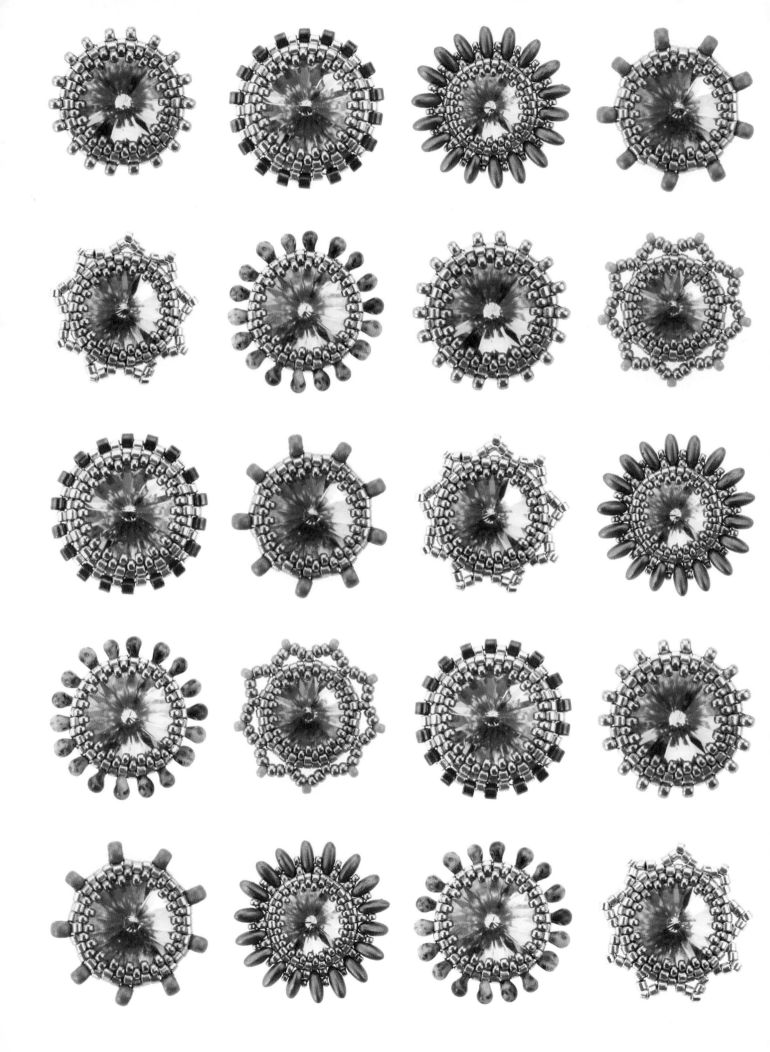

Basic Seed Bead Bezels

The simplest of techniques can make the most effective bezels so here are some ideas to experiment with...

Materials
Each bezel uses:
- 1 x 14mm Rivoli
- 1g of size 15 Miyuki seed beads - your S15 beads
- 1g of size 11 Cylinder beads - your C beads
- Optional - any extras such as drops, size 11 or 8 seed beads, size 10 Cylinder beads etc.

I used
- Rivolis: Light Turquoise
- Seed beads: Miyuki #4204 (size 15s) and #4203 (size 11s)
- Cylinder beads: DB1832

Techniques
- Stitch-In-The-Ditch, Page 11
- Basic Bezelling Technique, Page 12

> **TOP TIP**
> *You can also add a* **Star Design** *to any of these Rivolis*

> **TOP TIP**
> *SITD stands for Stitch-In-The-Ditch (see Page 11 for more information)*

Basic SITD

Simply adding SITD beads to your bezel gives you a decorative look. You can use cylinder beads to coordinate or seed beads, and different colours, for more of a contrast

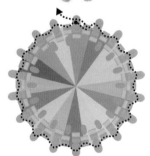

Extra Rounds

Your new SITD beads are perfect for beading into using Peyote Stitch. The space between the SITD beads is larger than what was in your bezel base and so you can use larger beads such as size 11 or 8 seeds or even size 10 cylinder beads as was used here

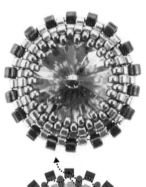

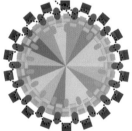

Spaced SITD

Adding SITD beads to alternate spaces on the central round of your bezel means you can use larger beads without worrying about them becoming too crowded

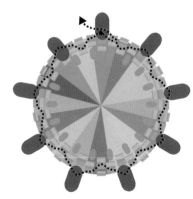

Basic Shapes

You can also use shaped beads, such as drops, for your SITD

 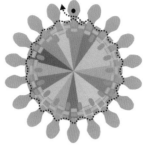

If they need reinforcement then you can weave around afterwards, adding new S15 or S11 beads, using Peyote Stitch, between each SITD bead

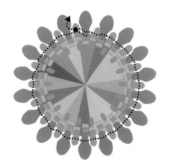

Deeper Shapes

If the shaped beads you're using have their holes further away from the ends then you can either add an extra round of beads first (as in **Extra Rounds SITD** on the previous page) or you can deepen the spaces by ladder-stitching S15 or S11 beads onto the SITD beads and then put the new beads into the spaces between them

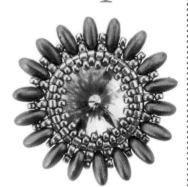

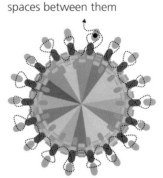 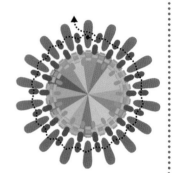

Loops

After you've added your SITD beads you can weave between them to add loops.
If you add an uneven number of beads in each loop then you can weave around again, missing out the central ones, pulling tight to make the central beads 'pop out'

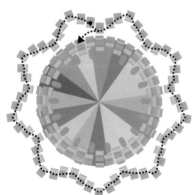 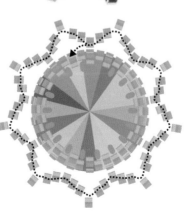

Loops with Seeds

Using seed beads, rather than cylinder beads, to make your loops gives you a softer look

Beaded Needle Case

Any of the bezels in this book which are based on the Basic Bezelling Technique can be used to make a needle case. Here I have made one with just some Stitch-In-The-Ditch for adornment

Materials
- 2 x 14mm Rivolis
- 1g of size 15 Miyuki seed beads - your S15 beads
- 4g of size 11 Cylinder beads - your C beads
- 1g size 11 seed beads - your S11 beads
- 1 x wooden needle case

I used
- Rivolis: Light Turquoise
- Seed beads: Miyuki #4204 (size 15s) and #4214 (size 11s)
- Cylinder beads: DB1832

Techniques
- Stitch-In-The-Ditch, Page 11
- Adding Star Designs, Page 16
- Peyote Stitch

THE LID
STEP 1
Bezelling the Rivoli.
Pick up 36 x C beads and circle through the first two to join into a ring. Using C beads add 1 more round and then 2 rounds of S15 beads pulling tight as you do so (54 x C and 36 x S15).

> **TOP TIP**
> *If needed you can use some double-sided sticky tape to secure your beadwork to the needle case or to 'pad out' the needle case if the beadwork is too loose on it*

STEP 2
If wanted add a **Star Design** to your rivoli.

STEP 3
Return to your tail thread, or weave your working thread to exit one of the C beads in the first round.

STEP 4
Using Peyote Stitch add 4 more rounds of C beads (18 x C per round).

STEP 5
Insert your Rivoli so it faces out of the S15 beads and then place the beadwork onto the lid of your needle case.

STEP 6
Using Peyote Stitch add as many rounds of C beads that are needed to bring your beadwork to the edge of the lid. As you add these rounds pull tight so that the beadwork 'bites' into the surface of the needle case.

THE EMBELLISHMENT
STEP 7
On the lid weave to exit a C bead in the second round of C beads from the front of the Rivoli. Using SITD add a round of S11s to your lid (18 x S11).

STEP 8
Weave to exit a C bead 3 rounds further down and add another round of S11s using SITD (18 x S11).

STEP 9
Repeat Step 8 once more and weave your thread away.

The Body
STEP 10
Repeat the principle of Steps 1-6 but adding a Rivoli and beadwork to the body of your needle case.

> **TOP TIP**
> *When adding the lid embellishment you can add extra rounds of SITD, or even leave it off completely, according to what you prefer*

Susie Qs

These sweet little stars are formed from just seed beads and are quick & easy to make

Materials

Each Susie Q uses:

- 1 x 14mm Rivoli
- 1g of size 15 Miyuki seed beads - S15s
- 1g of size 11 Miyuki seed beads - S11s
- 1g of size 8 seed beads (any brand seem to work) - S8s

I used (for the earrings shown)

- Rivoli: Olivine
- Seed beads: (15s & 11s) Miyuki #4206 (8s) Toho PF563

Techniques

- Peyote Stitch Decrease, Page 11

THE STEPS...

STEP 1

Starting the bezel

Pick up 5 x S8 and circle through the first to join into a circle. Pick up 3 x S11s. Repeat from * to * five more time to add six units in total and then finish by circling through the first S8 picked up and then the first S11 (30 x S8 and 18 x S11).

> **TOP TIP**
> *Your groups of S8 beads will now be referred to as 'Rings'*

> **TOP TIP**
> *From now on when you weave through what was a group of 3 x S11s you'll only thread through the 1st and 3rd one – don't thread through the 2nd one. This makes the centre one 'pop' and become a Picot*

STEP 2

Missing the 2nd S11 in the group of 3 thread into the 3rd and then into the 5th S8 picked up in the next Ring of S8s.
Pick up 3 x S11 and thread through the 2nd S8 picked up in the previous Ring, back through just 2 of your 3 x S11s and then thread through the 5th and 4th S8 picked up in the second Ring.
Pick up 3 x S11s and thread through the 3rd and 2nd S8 in this Ring and then the first S11 in the next group of 3 (6 x S11).

STEP 3

Repeat Step 2 five more times to add 10 more groups of 3 x S11 beads and at the end Step-Up to exit the 2nd S11 in the first group of 3 added in Step 2 (30 x S11).

STEP 4

Covering the Back.

This is covered using loops of S15s which thread into the centre bead in previous loops and pull them to the edge of your Rivoli. Once you've done each round you'll need to Step-Up to exit the central one in the first Loop.

- Pick up 7 x S15 and thread into the 2nd S11 in the next Picot which matches what you're exiting. Repeat five more times to add 6 loops (orange beads in the diagram).
- Insert your Rivoli so it faces out through your S8 beads.
- Add Loops of 3 x S15s between the centre beads in the 7-bead loop (the blue beads).
- Add single beads between each 3-bead loop (green beads).
- Add 1 x single bead and then, using a **Peyote Stitch Decrease**, decrease the next space. Repeat twice more, then when the round is done weave through these 3 beads to join (pink beads) (69 x S15).

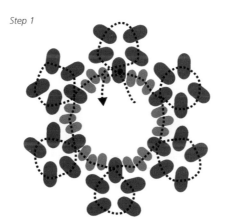

Step 1

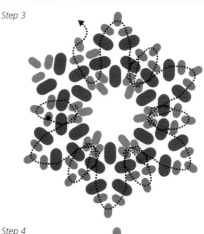

Step 3

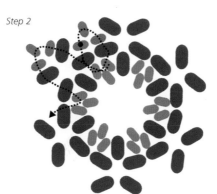

Step 2

Step 4

Star Flowers
Turn basic cylinder beads into striking bezels

Materials
Each Star Flower uses:
- 1 x 14mm Rivoli
- 1g of size 11 cylinder beads - C beads

I used
- Rivoli: Blush Rose
- Cylinder beads: DB2302, DB2285 and DB1832

Techniques
- Peyote Stitch Decrease, Page 11
- Stitch-In-The-Ditch, Page 11
- Peyote Stitch

THE STEPS...

STEP 1
Rounds 1-2 - The Base Circle.
Pick up 24 x C and circle through the first to join into a ring (24 x C).

STEP 2
Round 3.
Using Peyote Stitch, and beading into the Base Circle, add 2 x C into the first space and then 1 x C into the next. Repeat this pattern five more times and Step-Up at the end to 'split' the first pair added (18 x C).

STEP 3
Round 4.
Add 1 x C between the pair of C from the last round and then Peyote Stitch 1 x C into the next 2 spaces. Repeat from * to * five more times and then Step-Up to exit the first bead added (18 x C).

STEP 4
Round 5.
Using Peyote Stitch add 1 x C into each space between beads from the previous step (18 x C).

STEP 5
Round 6.
Using Peyote Stitch *add 1 x C into 2 spaces and then 2 x C into the next space*. Repeat from * to * five more times and then Step-Up to exit the first bead added (24 x C).

STEP 6
Round 7.
Using Peyote Stitch *Leave the next space empty by weaving through beads in previous rounds, then add 1 x C into 3 spaces*. Repeat from * to * five more times and then Step-Up to exit the first bead added (18 x C).

Step 1
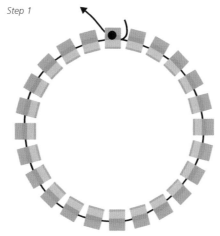

Step 2
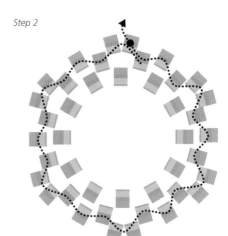

Step 3
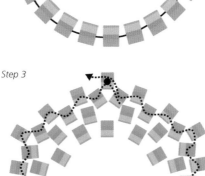

Step 4
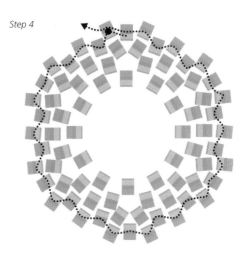

Step 5
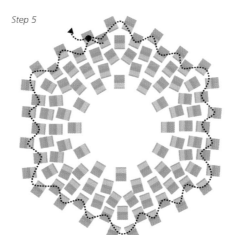

Step 6
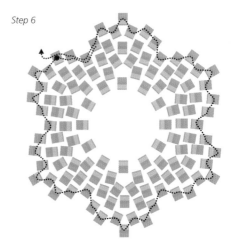

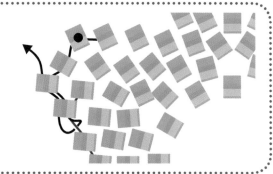

STEP 7

Using Peyote Stitch add 1 x C into 2 spaces and then turn to continue (2 x C).

STEP 8

Using Peyote Stitch add 2 x C into the space and then turn to continue (2 x C).

STEP 9

Add 1 x C into the space (splitting the pair added in the last step) and then weave through 6 more beads to the next Star Point ready to bead it (1 x C).

STEP 10

Repeat Steps 7-9 five more times so you bead each Star Point.

Step 7

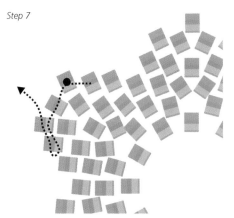

Step 8

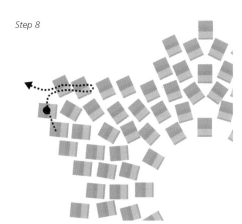

Step 9

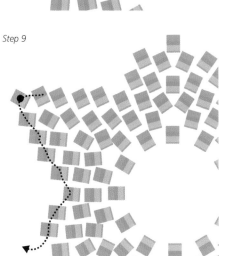

Step 10

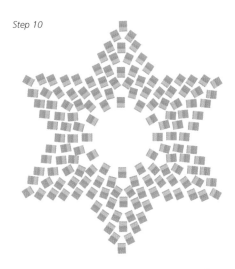

STEP 11
Beading the back – Round 1.
Weave to exit any bead added in Step 3 (Round 4 – the one where you split the pairs). Using **Stitch-In-The-Ditch** add 1 x C into each space on top of the beads in Round 4 (18 x C).

> **TOP TIP**
> *From now on exactly what you'll bead for each round will depend on where you wove to begin Step 11. The steps will detail the principle so pay attention to ensure you add the beads in the correct spots*

STEP 12
Beading the back – Round 2.
Using Peyote Stitch, and beading into all the beads added in the last step, add a round with 1 x C in each space (18 x C).

STEP 13
Beading the back – Round 3.
Using Peyote Stitch, and beading into all the beads added in the last step, add a round with 1 x C in each space (18 x C).

STEP 14
Insert your Rivoli so it faces out of the beads added in Steps 1-3.

STEP 15
Beading the back – Round 4.
Using Peyote Stitch you'll add 1 x C into the 2 'side' spaces and bead a **Peyote Stitch Decrease** in the 'corner' space which sits under the Star Point. Repeat this all the way around the round (12 x C).

STEP 16
Beading the back – Round 5.
Using Peyote Stitch you'll add 1 x C into each space including where you decreased in the last round (12 x C).

STEP 17
Beading the back – Round 6.
Using Peyote Stitch you'll add 1 x C into each space (12 x C).

STEP 18
Beading the back – Round 7.
Using Peyote Stitch you'll add 1 x C into 1 'side' space and bead a **Peyote Stitch Decrease** in the 'corner' space which sits under the Star Point. Repeat this all the way around the round (6 x C).

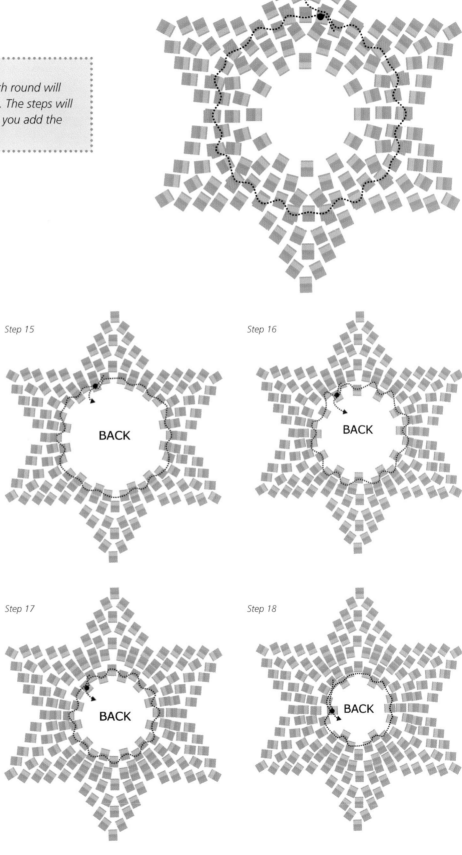

Step 11

Step 15

Step 16

Step 17

Step 18

BACK

STEP 19
Beading the back – Round 8.
Using Peyote Stitch add a round with 1 x C in each space (6 x C).

STEP 20
Beading the back – Round 9.
Using Peyote Stitch add a round with 1 x C in each space and then weave around the last 6 to unite (6 x C).

STEP 21
Optional extra bead.
If there's a space to fill at the back, then pick up 1 x C and circle through the opposite C bead from the last round, circle back the new C, and then circle back through the C you began this round exiting (1 x C).

STEP 22
Hanging Tab
The tab is made of a piece of Peyote Stitch which is 3 beads wide and 12 rows long. Begin it by weaving to exit a bead added in Step 13 which sits just before a corner space. Add 1 x C for the first Row and then 1 x C twice for the second Row. Repeat this pattern for 10 more rows and then zip to the appropriate beads added in Step 19 or 20 to secure and finish (18C).

> **TOP TIP**
> *See the* **Half Circle Teardrop Pendant** *for more information on beading a Hanging Tab*

Step 19

Step 20
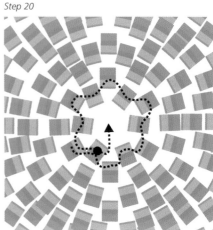

Step 21
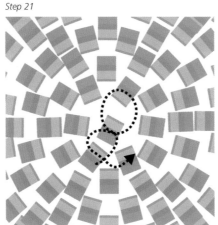

Step 22
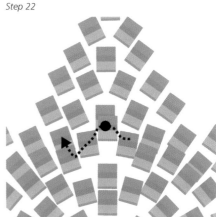

Variations

- Instead of beading individual Star Flowers you can join them into a chain which looks great as a bracelet. To do this begin a hanging tab (Step 22) and continue the Peyote Stitch to make a strip which you zip to another Star Flower, as shown in this diagram:

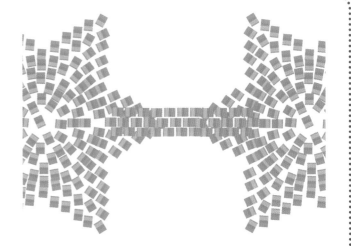

- Experiment with where you place different colours to completely change the look of your Star Flower

- As long as you bead the structural parts in cylinder beads (Steps 1-3 and 11-21) then the rest can be beaded in size 11 seed beads for a more rounded, textured look

- You can also bead tabs on the sides of your Star Flowers and link them as I did in my **Pearl Buds** necklace

More Elaborate Star Flower

STEP 1

Repeat Steps 1-8 of **Star Flowers** and then bead the equivalent of Step 9 but, as you thread through your work, just thread through 3 x C. Then pick up 6 x C and thread into the top C on the next Star Point (4 C beads away along the edge of the beadwork) to begin the next point (7C).

STEP 2

Continue beading all your points and adding 6 x C between them all the way around your work and then Step-Up to exit the first C bead in any of the 6 bead loops.

STEP 3

Ladder Stitch on 1 x C so that it sits, attached to the 1st bead in the loop, in the centre of the loop. Then, using Peyote Stitch, add 1 x C, then add 1 x C between the 3rd and 4th beads in the loop and then using Peyote Stitch add 1 more C. Lastly, Ladder Stitch the first bead added in this step to the 6th bead in the loop so that the new bead sits fully in the centre of what was a loop (4 x C).

STEP 4

Repeat Step 3 all around your Flower and then bead Steps 11-22 of **Star Flowers** to finish your work.

Step 2

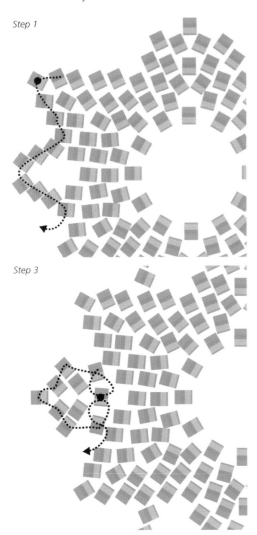
Step 1

Step 3

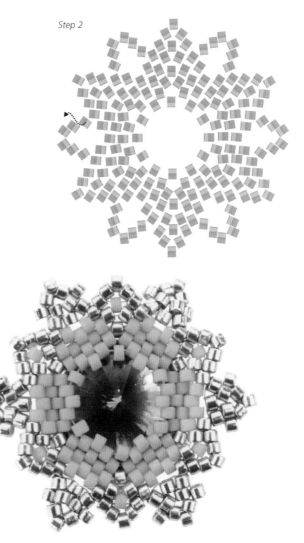

Crystal Cages
Quick to bead, and with lots of open spaces, these Bezels let your Rivolis shine through

This project has 2 variations – Single Strands (which show more of your Rivoli) and Double Strands (which use Herringbone Stitch and cover more of your Rivoli). You can mix & match them as desired

Materials
Each Crystal Cage uses:
- 1 x 14mm Rivoli
- 1g of size 11 Cylinder beads

I used
- Rivoli: Rose
- Cylinder beads: DB1831
- Clasp: Claspgarten 14551-01-06-00 in Rose

Techniques
- Peyote Stitch Decrease, Page 11
- Peyote Stitch
- Herringbone Stitch

SINGLE STRAND THE STEPS...
STEP 1
The Front – The First Unit.
Pick up 6C. Ignoring the last C (this becomes a 'Point Bead') thread back through the 5th and 4th and then circle through the 3rd (6 x C).

STEP 2
Units 2-6.
Repeat Step 1 five more times and then thread through the first 2C added in Step 1 to join into a circle and then weave to exit any Point Bead (30 x C).

STEP 3
The Back – Round 1.
Pick up 5 x C and thread into the next Point bead. Repeat 5 more times and then thread into the Point bead you began this step exiting and the first C bead picked up in this step (30 x C).

STEP 4
The Back – Round 2.
Insert your Rivoli so that it faces out from the beads added in Steps 1-2. *Peyote Stitch 2 single C beads and then bead a **Peyote Stitch Decrease** in the next space (which should line up with a Point Bead)*. Repeat from * to * five more times to finish the round and finish by Stepping-Up to exit the first bead added (12 x C).

STEP 5
The Back – Round 3.
Using Peyote Stitch add 1 x C in the first space and then add 2 x C in the next space (which should line-up with where you beaded a decrease in the last round). Repeat from * to * five more times to finish the round and finish by Stepping-Up to exit the first bead added (18 x C).

STEP 6
The Back – Round 4.
Pick up 3 x C and thread into the next single bead added in the last round*. Repeat from * to * five more times to finish the round and finish by Stepping-Up to exit the second bead added (18 x C).

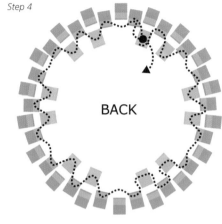

Step 4

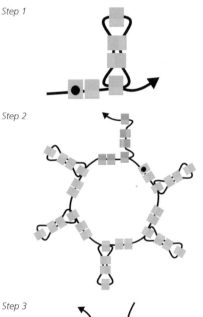

Step 1

Step 2

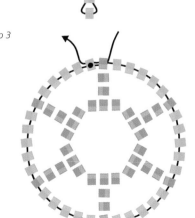

Step 3

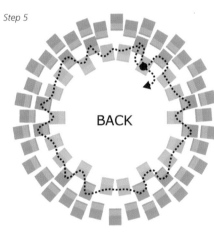

Step 5

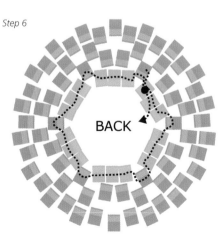

Step 6

Step 7

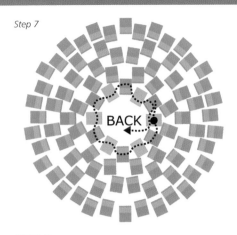

Step 8

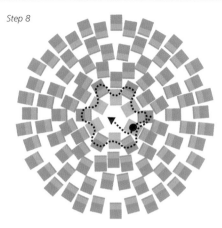

Step 9

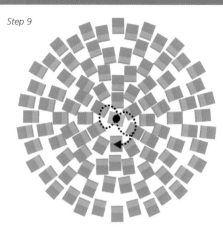

STEP 7

The Back – Round Five.

Pick up 1 x C and thread into the 2nd C bead in the next loop of 3C from the last round. Repeat from * to * five more times to finish the round and finish by Stepping-Up to exit the first bead added (6 x C).

STEP 8

The Back – Round Six.

Using Peyote Stitch add single C beads into each C from the last round (6 x C).

STEP 9

The Back – Round Seven.

Pick up 1 x C and circle through the opposite C bead from the last round, circle back through the new C, and then circle back through the C you began this round exiting (1 x C).

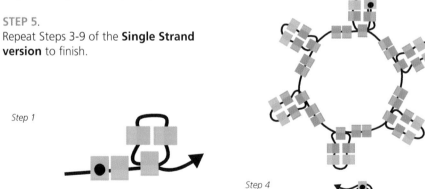

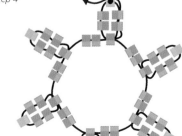

Variations

JOINING PIECES

If you want to join your pieces as you go then, as you bead Round Two of The Back, add 1 x C into 2 of the 6 spaces where you'd usually bead a decrease. If joining pieces in a line (as in the bracelet shown) then you want to do this on 2 spaces opposite each other (in this diagram the extra beads you'll add in are purple)

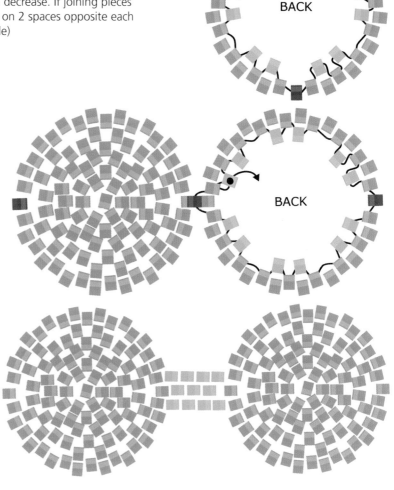

BACK

Then, when you bead your next component, and as you bead Round 2 of The Back, zip into one of these extra beads to join 2 Rivoli bezels together. Next, if you're continuing to make a line of bezels, add in an extra C opposite where you've zipped ready to join the next Rivoli onto

BACK

You can also bead a **Beaded Tab** (see Page 20) from the edge of a piece using Odd-Count Peyote Stitch which then zips to another Crystal Cage to unite them or use tabs to join bezels and Beaded Links as used in the **Pearl Buds** necklace

You could also use pieces of Right-Angle Weave to join different Cages together

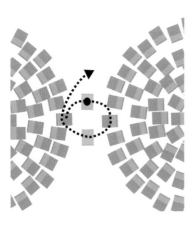

MAKING EARRINGS OR PENDANTS

These bezels can be hung from loops of S or C beads from any of the Point Beads

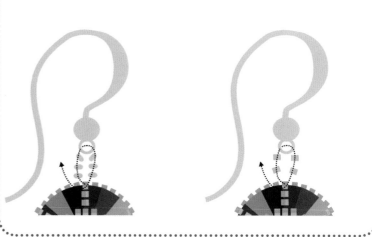

Honeycomb

Subtle geometric shapes allow a Rivoli's colour & sparkle to shine out!

Using 2 sizes of seed beads to create bezels allows you to create a geometric shape with a softer look

Materials

Each single Rivoli uses:
- 1 x 14mm Rivoli
- 1g size 15 Miyuki seed beads in Main Colour – your 15M beads
- 6 or 12 x Miyuki size 15 seed beads in Highlight Colour – your 15H beads
- 24 x size 11 Miyuki seed beads in Highlight Colour – your S11 beads

I used

- Rivolis: Padparadscha, Topaz, and Sunflower
- Seed beads: Miyuki #4202 (Highlight) and #4202F (Main)
- Clasp: Claspgarten 14551-01-01-00-203 in Topaz

Techniques

- Ladder Stitch

THE STEPS...

STEP 1

First round

Pick up 1 x S11 and 1 x 15H. Circle through the S11 and then pick up 6 x 15M (1 x S11, 1 x 15H and 6 x 15M).

STEP 2

Repeat Step 1 five more times to have a total of 6 units of beads and then circle through the first S11 to join into a ring (5 x S11, 5 x 15H and 30 x 15M).

STEP 3.

Second Round

Thread into a 15H (changing direction as you do so) and then *pick up 5 x 15M. Thread into the next 15H*.

Repeat from * to * 5 more times to add a complete round of 6 groups of 5 x 15M (30 x 15M).

STEP 4

Beginning the Third Round

Weave to exit a S11 added in Step 1 or 2. *Using Ladder Stitch add 1 x S11 to this bead. Thread through 6 x 15M to get to the next S11* and repeat from * to * five more times to complete the round (6 x S11)

STEP 5

Completing the Third Round

Step-up to exit any of the S11 beads added in the last step. *Pick up 5 x 15M and thread into the next S11 added in the last step pulling tight as you go*.

Repeat from * to * 5 more times to add 6 units of 5 x 15M (30 x 15M).

TOP TIP

There's a lot of changing direction in this project!

Step 1

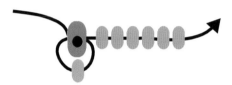

Step 2

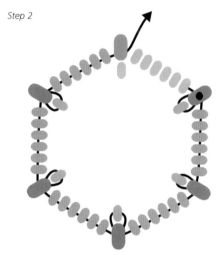

Step 3

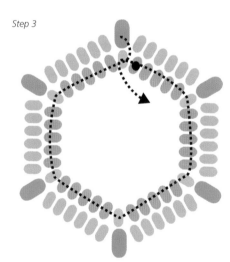

Step 4

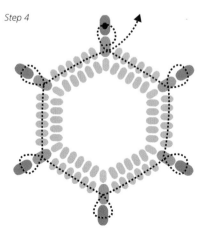

Step 5

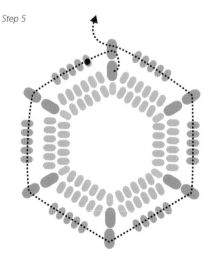

TOP TIP

I like to do a lot of weaving around my work to keep the beads tight and straight but you may want to save this until you have beaded the bezel and know you can fit through the beads multiple times – the choice is yours

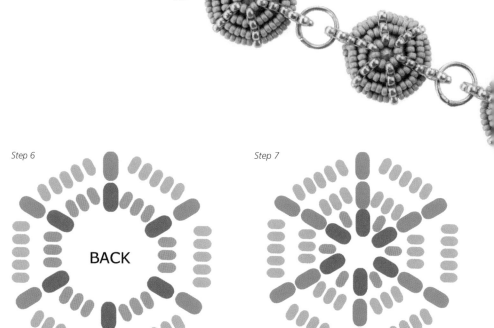

STEP 6

The Fourth Round

Insert your Rivoli so that the front faces out through the beads added in Steps 1-3. Repeat the principle of Steps 4-5 to add a round of S11s Ladder-Stitched onto the previous S11s and groups of 3 x 15M between each one (6 x S11 and 18 x 15M).

STEP 7

The Fifth Round

Repeat the principle of Step 6 to add a round of S11s Ladder-Stitched onto the previous S11s and groups of 1 x 15M between each one (6 x S11 and 6 x 15M).

STEP 8

Finishing the Bezel.

Weave through all the 15M beads added in the Fifth Round to secure and finish your thread.

Step 6

BACK

Step 7

Variations

HONEYCOMB VARIATION

If you'd like to do extra beading, which covers the front of your Rivoli more, then after Step 3, repeat the principles of Steps 2-3 to Ladder-Stitch on 1 x 15H to each 15H in the last round and then fill in between them with 3 x 15M

BEADED LINKS

If you want to link your Honeycombs together then, after beading Step 4 or 5, you can Ladder-Stitch on a chain of 4 x S11s (or more beads if you want larger loops) joined to two S11s which sit next to each other. This gives you a loop you can thread a jump ring through

Extra Decoration

If you'd like to add extra decoration to your Honeycombs then you can 'loop' 3 x S11s or 3 x 15H onto each of your S11s from Steps 1-2

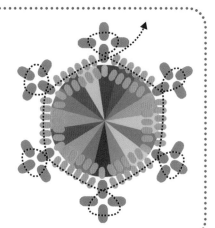

Making earrings & pendants

These bezels can be hung from loops of S15s or S11s from any of the S11s added in Step 1

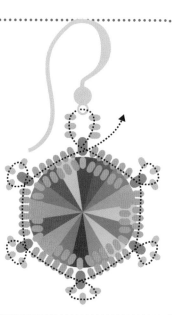

Joining Honeycombs

- If you'd like to join your Honeycombs directly to one another you can either do it by sharing an S11 from a previous Honeycomb as you bead Step 2 of your new Honeycomb...

- ...Or you can share some of the 15M beads from a previous Honeycomb as you bead Step 2

- You can also use RAW as shown on Page 21

Pearls

Discover the fun of adding a
touch of luxury to your Rivoli
beadwork...

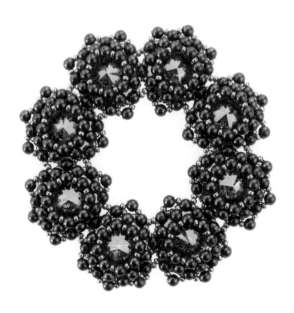

RAW Pearls Bezel
Combine Rivolis, Pearls and Right-Angle Weave for a wide variety of dazzling projects

Right-Angle Weave (RAW) with pearls is a beautiful way to make sophisticated and adorned bezels for your Rivolis

The Basics
These bezels use a variation of RAW with small seed beads and Pearls to hold each Rivoli in a simple yet elegant way

Materials
Each single RAW Pearl uses:
- 1 x 14mm Rivoli
- 1g of size 15 Miyuki seed beads - your S15 beads
- 24 x 3mm Swarovski Round Pearls #5810 - your P beads

I used
For my Original Version and Variation Two I used:
- Rivolis: Padparadscha
- Seed beads: Miyuki #4204
- Pearls: Swarovski Crystal Coral

Techniques
- Peyote Stitch Decrease, Page 11
- Right-Angle Weave (RAW)
- Peyote Stitch
- Netting

THE STEPS...
Original Version
The Original version uses small seed beads and Pearls to bezel Rivolis leaving as much of the sparkling front uncovered as possible.

STEP 1
Base Circle – first unit.
Pick up 1 x S15, 1P, 1 x S15 and 3 x P. Circle through the first 4 beads to join into a ring and to be ready to continue. Your first unit has P beads for 3 of its sides and 1 x S15, 1P and 1 x S15 for its topmost side which will sit on the outer edge of the Base Circle (2 x S15, 4 x P).

STEP 2
Continuing the RAW.
Using RAW continue adding units with just P beads on 3 sides and 1 x S15, 1P and 1 x S15 on their outer edge matching the first unit. Stop when you have 7 units completed (12 x S15 and 18 x P).

STEP 3
Finishing the Base Circle.
Using RAW add 1 final unit which matches the others to join your work into a circle with the sides containing S15s on the outer edge (2 x S15, 2 x P).

STEP 4
Weave to exit any P bead on the inner edge of your Base Circle. *Pick up 1 x S15 and thread into the next P on the inner edge. Repeat from * to * seven more times to add a total of 8 x S15 beads and weave all around the thread-path to secure and pull tight (8 x S15).

> **TOP TIP**
> *For some of the projects you may need a stronger thread than usual as it will be pulled across the sharp edges of the Pearls multiple times so something like Fireline may be best. However, for projects where the work is pulled together tightly (e.g. when 2 Pearls are shared between bezels such as in the **Rachel Pendant**), you may need a flexible thread*

Step 1

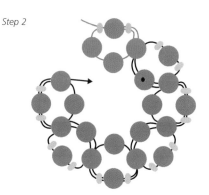

Step 2

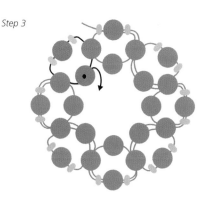

Step 3

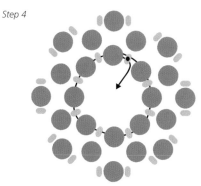

Step 4

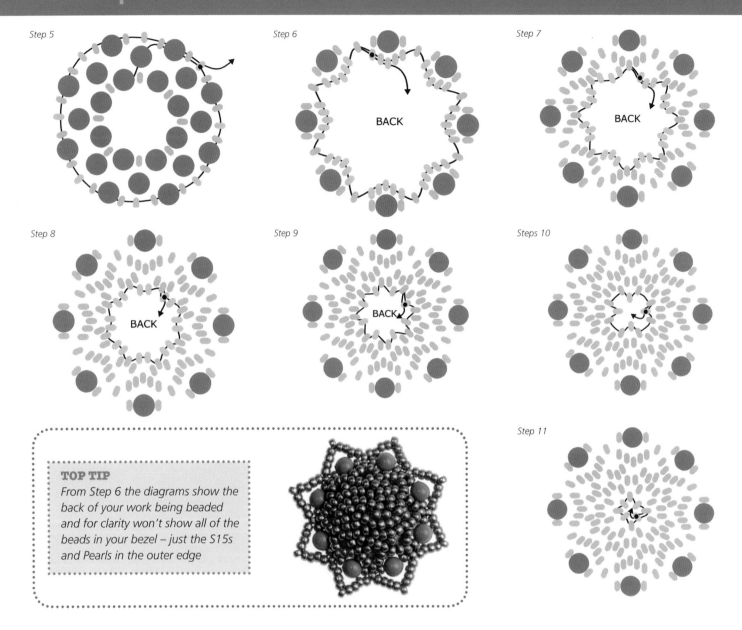

Step 5

Step 6

BACK

Step 7

BACK

Step 8

BACK

Step 9

BACK

Steps 10

Step 11

TOP TIP
From Step 6 the diagrams show the back of your work being beaded and for clarity won't show all of the beads in your bezel – just the S15s and Pearls in the outer edge

STEP 5
The Back - Round 1.
Weave to exit any S15 on the outer edge AFTER a P bead. *Pick up 1 x S15 and thread through the next S15, P and S15 on the outer edge of the next unit*. Repeat from * to * seven more times. Step-Up at the end of the round to exit the first S15 added in this step (8 x S15).

STEP 6
Round 2.
Pick up 5 x S15 and thread into the next S15 bead added in the last step. Repeat from * to * seven more times and Step-Up at the end to exit the 3rd bead added in this step (40 x S15).

STEP 7
Round 3.
Insert your Rivoli so it faces out of the beadwork added in Steps 1- 4. *Pick up 3 x S15 and thread into the 3rd bead in the next loop added in the last round*. Repeat from * to * seven more times and Step-Up to exit the 2nd bead added in the 1st loop in this step (24 x S15).

STEP 8
Round 4.
Add a round with loops of 2 x S15s threading into the 2nd S15 in each loop from the last round. At the end of the round Step-Up to exit the 1st bead added in the 1st loop (16 x S15).

STEP 9
Round 5.
Using Peyote Stitch add 1 x S15 and thread into the 1st bead in the next loop added in the last round. Repeat seven more times and at the end of the round Step-Up to exit the first bead added (8 x S15).

STEP 10
Round 6.
Using Peyote Stitch add 1 x S15 and then, using a **Peyote Stitch Decrease,** decrease the next space. Repeat this pattern 3 more times and finish the round by Stepping-Up to exit the first bead added (4 x S15).

STEP 11
Round 7.
Add 1 x S15 bead between each bead added in the last round and then weave through all 4 new beads to secure (4 x S15).

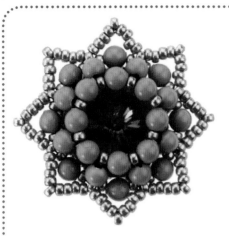

VARIATION ONE

This variation adds Star Points around each pearl in the outer edge for extra visual texture. These Star Points are created by first adding loops of beads and then weaving through those loops but ignoring the central bead to form the 'points'

Step 2

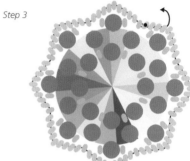

I used

- Rivolis: Padparadscha
- Seed beads: Miyuki #4204
- Pearls: Crystal Turquoise

STEP 1
Bead Steps 1-11 of the **RAW Pearls Bezel - Original Version**.

STEP 2
You'll now add extra S15 beads along the outside edge. These will sit in the same position as those added in the 1st round of the back of the bezel you beaded.
Weave to exit any S15 on the outer edge AFTER a P bead. *Pick up 1 x S15 and thread through the next S15, P and S15 on the edge of the next unit*.
Repeat from * to * seven more times. Step-Up at the end of the round to exit the first S15 added (8 x S15).

Step 3

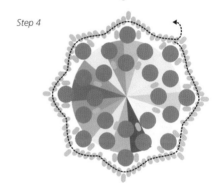

STEP 3
You're now going to add loops of beads. Pick up 9 x S15 and thread into the next S15 added in the last round. Repeat seven more times to add 8 loops of beads. Step-Up at the end of the round to exit the 4th bead added in the 1st loop (72 x S15).

Step 4

STEP 4
You'll now weave through again to make the central beads 'pop' out.
Missing the 5th bead in the loop thread through the next 4 x S15s in the loop, the next S15 added in Step 2 and the first 4 x S15 beads added in the next loop. Repeat from * to * pulling tight to make all the 5th beads in the loops 'pop out' to form points.

VARIATION TWO

This variation adds 'Spikes' between each pearl in the outer circle for extra interest

STEP 1
Bead Steps 1-11 of the **RAW Pearls Bezel - Original Version**.

STEP 2
Weave to exit any S15 on the outer edge AFTER a P bead facing towards the next P. *Pick up 3 x S15 and, missing the last 1, thread back down 1. Pick up 1 x S15 and thread through the next S15, P and S15 on the edge of the next unit*. Repeat from * to * seven more times to complete the round (32 x S15).

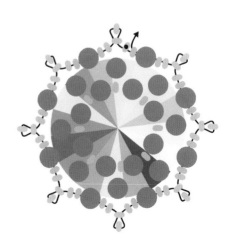

Making a larger RAW Pearl Bezel
If you want to bezel a 27mm #1201 Swarovski crystal (or similar) then you need to adapt the basic bezel by adding more units

The principle of what you're beading is exactly the same, but there will be 16 units around the crystal rather than the 8 which you have in the 14mm Rivoli bezels and there are more rounds of beadwork to cover the back (optional – you can stop as soon as your crystal is secure)

Materials
- 1 x 27mm Swarovski Crown Stone #1201 or similar
- 3g of size 15 Miyuki seed beads - your S15 beads
- 48 x 3mm Swarovski Round Pearls #5810 - your P beads

Techniques
- Peyote Stitch Decrease, Page 11
- Right-Angle Weave (RAW)
- Peyote Stitch
- Netting

THE STEPS...

STEP 1
The Base Circle - first unit.
Pick up 1 x S15, 1P, 1 x S15 and 3 x P. Circle through the first 4 beads to join into a ring. Your first unit has P beads for 3 of its sides and 1 x S15, 1P and 1 x S15 for its topmost side which will sit on the outer edge of the Base Circle (2 x S15, 4 x P).

STEP 2
Continuing the RAW.
Using RAW continue adding units with just P beads on 3 sides and 1 x S15, 1P and 1 x S15 on their outer edge matching the first unit. Stop when you have 15 units completed (28 x S15 and 42 x P).

STEP 3
Finishing the Base Circle.
Using RAW add 1 final unit which matches the others to join your work into a circle with the sides containing S15s on the outer edge (2 x S15, 2 x P).

STEP 4
Weave to exit any P bead on the inner edge of your circle.
Pick up 1 x S15 and thread into the next P. Repeat from * to * to add a total of 16 x S15 beads and weave all around the thread-path to secure and pull tight (16 x S15).

Step 2

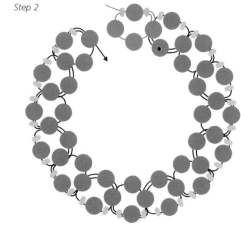

Step 1

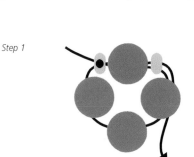

Step 3

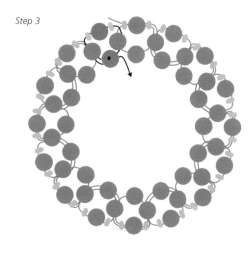

Step 4

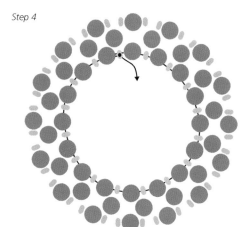

STEP 5

The Back - Round 1.
Weave to exit any S15 on the outer edge AFTER a P bead. *Pick up 1 x S15 and thread through the next S15, P and S15 on the edge of the next unit*. Repeat from * to * fifteen more times. Step-Up at the end of the round to exit the first S15 added in this step (16 x S15).

STEP 6

Round 2.
Pick up 5 x S15 and thread into the next S15 bead added in the last step. Repeat from * to * fifteen more times and Step-Up at the end to exit the 3rd bead added in this step (80 x S15).

STEP 7

Round 3.
Insert your crystal so it faces out of the beadwork added in Steps 1-4. *Pick up 5 x S15 and thread into the 3rd bead in the next loop added in the last round*. Repeat from * to * fifteen more times and Step-Up to exit the 3rd bead added in the 1st loop in this step (80 x S15).

STEP 8

Round 4.
Add a round with loops of 3 x S15s threading into the 3rd S15 in each loop from the last round. At the end of the round Step-Up to exit the 2nd bead added in the 1st loop (48 x S15).

STEP 9

Round 5.
Add a round with loops of 3 x S15s threading into the 2nd S15 in each loop from the last round. At the end of the round Step-Up to exit the 1st bead added in the 1st loop (48 x S15).

STEP 10

Round 6.
Add a round with loops of 2 x S15s threading into the 2nd S15 in each loop from the last round. At the end of the round Step-Up to exit the 1st bead added in the 1st loop (32 x S15).

STEP 11

Round 7.
Using Peyote Stitch add 1 x S15 between the 2 x S15s where you are (splitting the pair of beads) and then, using a **Peyote Stitch Decrease,** decrease the next space. Repeat this pattern 15 more times and finish the round by Stepping-Up to exit the first bead added (16 x S15).

Step 5

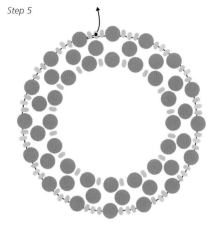

TOP TIP
These instructions for covering the back describe what I did but you may need to vary it depending on the size of the S15 beads you use

Step 6

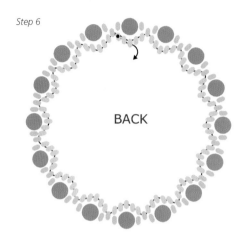

BACK

Step 7

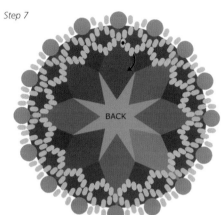

BACK

Step 8

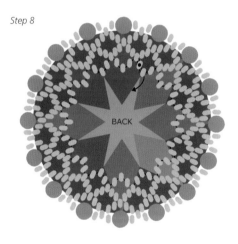

BACK

Step 9

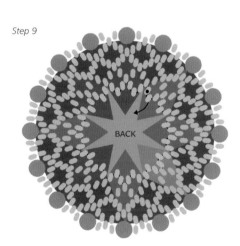

BACK

Step 10

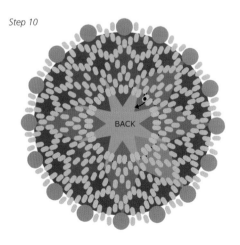

BACK

Step 11

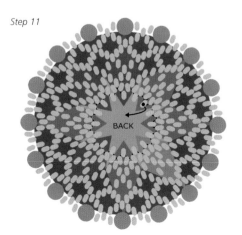

BACK

STEP 12
Round 8.
Using Peyote Stitch add 1 x S15 between each bead added in the last round. At the end of the round Step-Up to exit the first bead added (16 x S15).

STEP 13
Round 9.
Using Peyote Stitch add 1 x S15 and then, using a **Peyote Stitch Decrease**, decrease the next space. Repeat this pattern seven more times and finish the round by Stepping-Up to exit the first bead added (8 x S15).

STEP 14
Round 10.
Using Peyote Stitch add 1 x S15 and then, using a **Peyote Stitch Decrease**, decrease the next space. Repeat this pattern 3 more times and finish the round by Stepping-Up to exit the first bead added (4 x S15).

STEP 15
Round 11.
Using Peyote Stitch add 1 x S15 between each bead added in the last round and then weave all around the 4 beads to tie them together (4 x S15).

Step 12
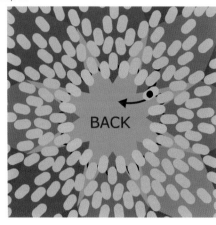

Step 13

Step 14
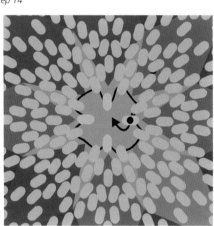

Step 15
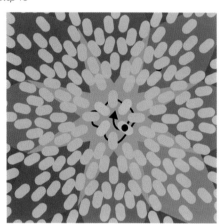

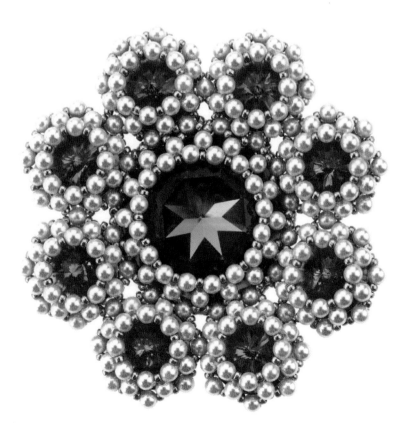

Subsequent RAW Pearl Bezels
The next step after making RAW Pearl Bezels is growing other ones directly from them...

Growing 1 RAW Pearls Bezel directly from another instantly opens up a world of new projects & adventures

There are numerous ways you can begin a new **RAW Pearls Bezel**. The first is beading a new single **RAW Pearls Bezel** (any of the variations) but that only gives you individually made bezelled Rivolis. As soon as you want to make pieces with multiple bezelled Rivolis you need to 'grow them' from previous ones in either of 2 ways:

- **GROWN DIRECTLY FROM PEARLS**
  This is the most commonly used method in all the projects. It has subsequent bezels growing from a Pearl on the outer edge of another bezel. The 2 bezels will share 1 or 2 P beads between them depending on what you're beading

- **GROWN FROM SEED BEADS**
  This method is used when you need to bead the back of the bezel first as you won't be able to get to it afterwards (i.e. when making a 3D shape).
  Subsequent bezels will share 1 or 2 Pearls with previous ones depending on what you're making
  The end results are almost the same (the only difference is the back of the 'Grown from Seeds' versions is not fully covered) and they can each share 1 or 2 Pearls between bezels

TOP TIP
If your bezels share just 1 Pearl then the connection will be looser and more flexible. If they share 2 Pearls the connection will be tighter and the work will 'cup' more. When making a piece that shares 2 Pearls you may want to use a more flexible thread that has some stretch and give in it

Grown From Pearls

These bezels are begun directly from Pearls on your previous bezel and are beaded using exactly the same principle, they just use 1 or 2 fewer Pearls in each bezel

SHARING 1 PEARL...
STEP 1
Using your variation of choice bead a RAW Pearls bezel with a Rivoli in it. Weave to exit any Pearl on the outer edge of your bezel.

STEP 2
Beading the 1st unit of the 2nd bezel. Pick up 1 x S15, 3P and 1 x S15. Circle through the P you were exiting to make the unit and then the 1st S15 and P you picked up to be ready to continue (2 x S15, 3P).

Steps 1-2

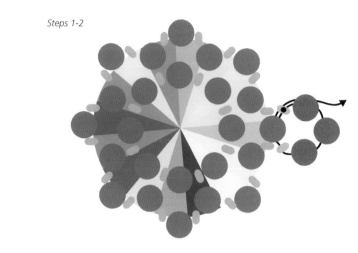

STEP 3
Continue beading your bezel as usual but treating the 'shared' Pearl as belonging to this new bezel (14 x S15, 20P).

Step 3

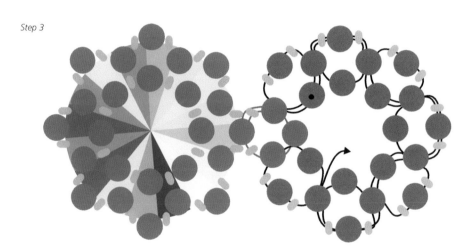

SHARING 2 PEARLS...
STEP 1
If your project has 2 Pearls shared between bezels then, when beading both the 1st and 2nd unit of the second bezel, you'll pick up 1 less Pearl and instead thread through Pearls in the previous bezel making them shared between the bezels. When you bead this it will pull your work, and your beadwork will no longer lay completely flat as you continue the next bezel.

Step 1

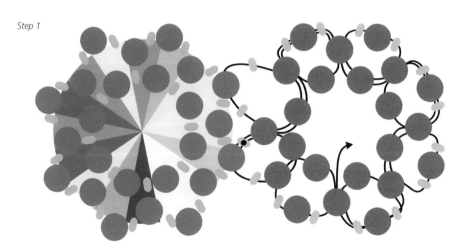

Grown From Seeds

These bezels are begun with Seed Beads and you start by beading the back of the bezel working towards the front. This method is used when what you're making means you won't be able to access the back of the bezel to decrease i.e. in **RAW Pearls Scarf Ring** or **Josephine Pendant**

SINGLE BEZEL..
STEP 1
Base Strand.
Pick up 24 x S15 beads and circle through the 1st one to join into a circle (24 x S15).

STEP 2
Netting with 3 beads.
Pick up 3 x S15 and, missing 2 x S15 beads on your Base Strand, thread into the next. Repeat this pattern all around your Base Strand and finish by Stepping-Up to exit the 2nd bead added in this round (24 x S15).

STEP 3
Netting with 5 beads.
Pick up 5 x S15 and thread into the 2nd S15 on the next loop of 3 x S15 beads picked up in the last step. Repeat this pattern all the way around and finish by Stepping-Up to exit the 3rd bead added in this round (40 x S15).

STEP 4
Edge of RAW Units.
Pick up 1 x S15, 1 P and 1 x S15. Thread into the 3rd S15 of the 5-bead loop added in the last step. Repeat this pattern all the way around and Step-Up to exit the first group of 3 beads added in this round (16 x S15, 8P).

STEP 5
Finishing the bezel.
Add your Rivoli so that the back sits on the beads added in Steps 1-3. Then, working into the groups of 3 beads added in the last step, turn them into the outer edges of 8 RAW units. Then add in the 8 x S15 beads which sit between RAW units at the inner edge of the bezel (8 x S15, 16 x P).

SUBSEQUENT BEZELS...
STEP 1
When making subsequent bezels, at Step 4 you'll need to pick up 1 (or 2) fewer Pearls and instead use a Pearl in the previous bezel.

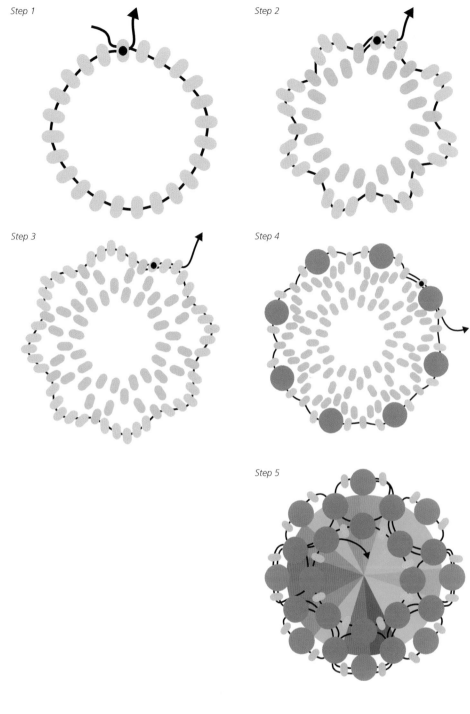

Step 1

Step 2

Step 3

Step 4

Step 5

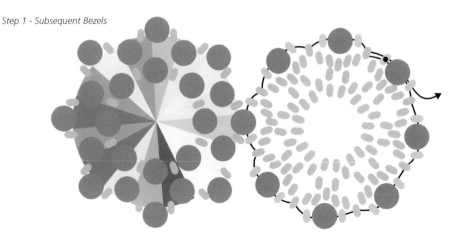

Step 1 - Subsequent Bezels

Annetta Pendant

This pendant is formed of 3 bezelled Rivolis joined together with a large drop pendant hanging from them. It can be worn as either a brooch or a pendant depending on your choice on the day

Materials
- 3 x 14mm Rivolis
- 2g of size 15 Miyuki seed beads - your S15 beads
- 68 x 3mm Swarovski Round Pearls #5810 - your P beads
- 1 x 32mm Swarovski Ellipse Drop Pendant #6470 or similar

I used
- Rivolis: Olivine
- Seed beads: Miyuki #4204
- Pearls: Crystal Vintage Gold
- Pendant Drop: Olivine

Techniques
- RAW Pearls Bezel - Original Version, Page 46
- Grown From Pearls, Page 54
- Right-Angle Weave
- Peyote Stitch

THE STEPS...

STEP 1
The 1st Bezel.
Bead a Rivoli using Steps 1-11 of **The Raw Pearls Bezel - Original Version**. To finish weave to exit any P on the outer edge of the bezel.

STEP 2
The 2nd Bezel.
Using the **Grown From Pearls** method add a 2nd bezel to the 1st making sure it shares 2 Pearls in the original bezel. This 2nd one can be added to any of the pairs of Pearls next to each other in the 1st bezel.

STEP 3
The 3rd Bezel.
Decide what will be the Inner & outer edges of your pendant and add 1 more bezel using the **Grown From Pearls** method (sharing 2 Pearls) making sure that this one is spaced so that there are 4 free Pearls on the outer edge of your 2nd bezel and NO free Pearls on the inner edge.

STEP 4
Adding the drop.
You can add this in a few different ways but here is what I did:
- Weave to exit the first 'unshared' pearl on the outer edge of either of your edge bezels on the pendant. Make sure you're facing away from the group of bezels.
- Pick up 8 x S15s and the Drop Pendant (4 x S15s will sit inside the hole in the Drop Pendant) and thread into the equivalent Pearl on the other edge bezel again facing towards the group of bezels.
- Weave through your work to exit the next Pearl on the other edge of this bezel facing towards the Drop Pendant.
- Pick up 3 x S15 and thread through the central 4 x S15s added in the first loop.
- Pick up 3 x S15s and thread up through the next Pearl on the original bezel facing away from the body of the Pendant.

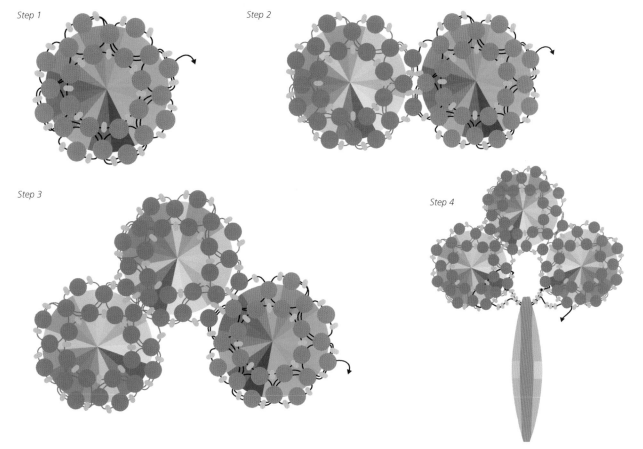

Step 1

Step 2

Step 3

Step 4

STEP 5

Hanging Loop.

Weave to exit any S15 bead sitting near the centre of your central bezel.

Pick up 23 x S15 (you can use more or less if you know what size your stringing materials will be – the diagram shows fewer than this) and thread into any S15 bead at the back of the same bezel towards the bottom/ inner edge. Weave back and forth through this thread-path to secure (23 x S15).

Step 5

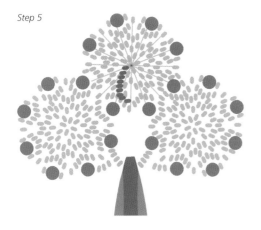

Variations

- Instead of using a large drop you could add multiple swags of S15s and Pearls or bicone crystals

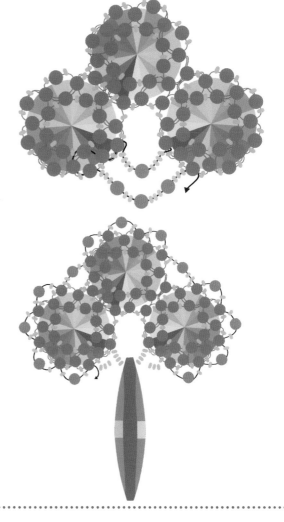

- You could also add the Outer Edge Embellishment from Step 5 of the **Jo Ellen Pendant** to your 3 bezels. You may need to experiment with what beads you use to bridge between the bezels

- You can use any of the **RAW Pearls Bezel** variations to add extra decoration to the edges but you may need to adjust the embellishment where the bezels meet each other

Rachel Pendant

The Basics

This pendant is formed of 4 bezelled Rivolis with each one joined to 2 others and sharing 2 Pearls with each of those. The addition of 2 hanging loops means that the pendant can be worn in 2 different ways; as a square or as a diamond.

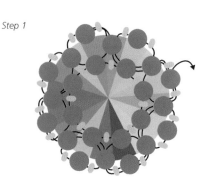

Step 1

Materials

- 4 x 14mm Rivolis
- 2g of size 15 Miyuki seed beads - your S15 beads
- 88 x 3mm Swarovski Round Pearls #5810 - your P beads

I used

- Rivolis: Padparadscha
- Seed beads: Miyuki #4203
- Pearls: Crystal Coral

Techniques

- RAW Pearls Bezel - Original Version, Page 46
- Grown From Pearls, Page 54
- Right-Angle Weave
- Peyote Stitch

> **TOP TIP**
> *After Step 3 your group of bezels now won't lie flat – this is to be expected*

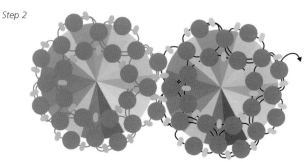

Step 2

THE STEPS...

STEP 1

The 1st Bezel.
Bead a Rivoli using Steps 1-11 of **The RAW Pearls Bezel - Original Version**. To finish weave to exit any P on the outer edge of the bezel.

STEP 2

The 2nd Bezel.
Using the **Grown From Pearls** method add a 2nd bezel to the first one making sure it shares 2 Pearls in the original bezel. This 2nd one can be added to any of the pairs of Pearls next to each other in the 1st bezel.

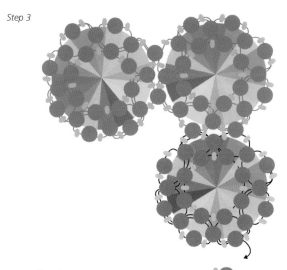

Step 3

STEP 3

The 3rd Bezel.
Decide what will be the inner & outer edges of your pendant and add 1 more bezel using the **Grown From Pearls** method (sharing 2 Pearls) making sure that each one is now spaced so that there are 4 free Pearls on the outer edge of your pendant and NO free Pearls on the inner edge.

STEP 4

The 4th Bezel.
Add a final bezel making sure to join it to both your 3rd and 1st bezels so that there are still 4 free Pearls on the outer edge of your circle and NO free Pearls on the inner edge.

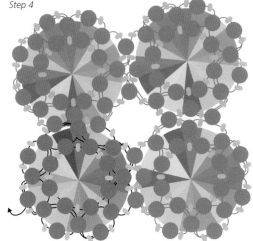

Step 4

STEP 5

Hanging Loops.

You can add 1 or 2 hanging loops to the back of your work. Having 2 allows the pendant to be hung in 2 different ways (as a diamond or as a square).

Weave to exit any S15 bead sitting near the centre of any of your bezels at the back.

Pick up 23 x S15 (you can use more or less if you know what size your stringing materials will be – the diagram shows fewer than this) and thread into any S15 bead at the back of the same bezel towards the bottom/ inner edge. Weave back and forth through this thread-path to secure (23 x S15 per loop).

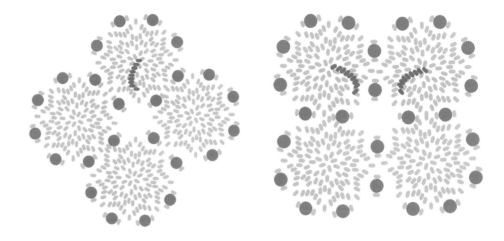

Variations

- You can hang a large drop using S15 beads either from one single Rivoli or bridged between 2 Rivolis. Experiment with different numbers of S15s to attach it and different attaching points to get the look you want

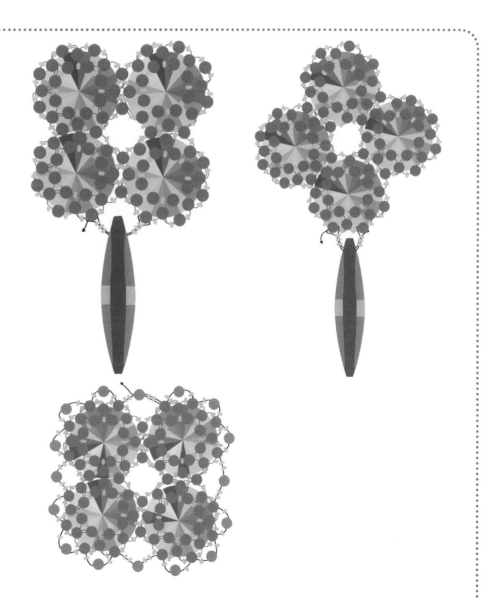

- You could also add the Outer Edge Embellishment from Step 5 of the **Jo Ellen Pendant** to your 4 bezels. You may need to experiment with what beads you use to bridge between the bezels

- You can use any of the **RAW Pearls Bezel** variations but you may need to adjust the embellishment where the bezels meet

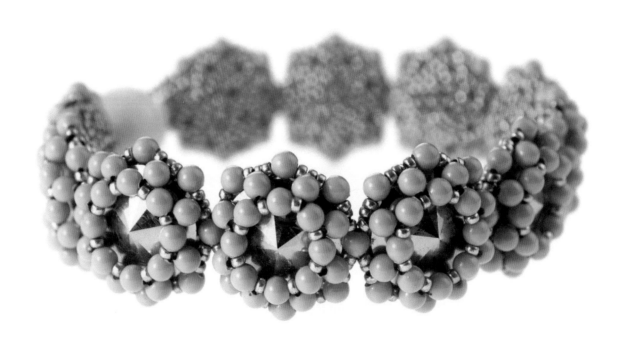

Sally Bracelet

This bracelet is formed of multiple bezelled Rivolis with each one growing directly from the previous one in a line before a clasp is added

Materials

For a 21cm / 8 ¼ inch bracelet
- 11 x 14mm Rivolis
- 6g of size 15 Miyuki seed beads - your S15 beads
- 254 x 3mm Swarovski Round Pearls #5810 - your P beads
- Clasp of choice - I used a 12mm magnetic clasp to match my Pearls

I used

- Rivolis: Crystal Rose Gold
- Seed beads: Miyuki #4221
- Pearls: Crystal Turquoise

Techniques

- RAW Pearls Bezel - Original Version, Page 46
- Grown From Pearls, Page 54
- Right-Angle Weave
- Peyote Stitch

THE STEPS...

STEP 1

The first Bezel.
Leaving a thread tail, which you'll use to later attach your clasp, bezel a Rivoli using Steps 1-11 of **The RAW Pearls Bezel - Original Version**.

STEP 2

The Second Bezel.
Weave to exit any P in the outer edge and using the **Grown From Pearls** method add a 2nd bezel to the 1st making sure it shares just 1 Pearl. This 2nd one can be added to any of the Pearls in the 1st bezel.

STEP 3

Subsequent Bezels.
Continue adding bezels using the **Grown From Pearls** method making sure that each one now begins from the Pearl directly opposite the one shared with a previous bezel and only shares 1 Pearl. Do this until the bracelet is almost as long as needed, allowing for the clasp.

Step 1

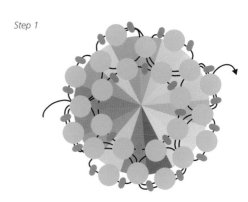

Step 2

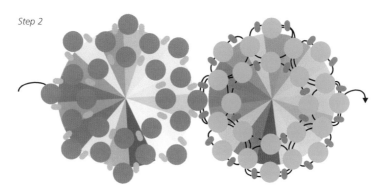

Step 3

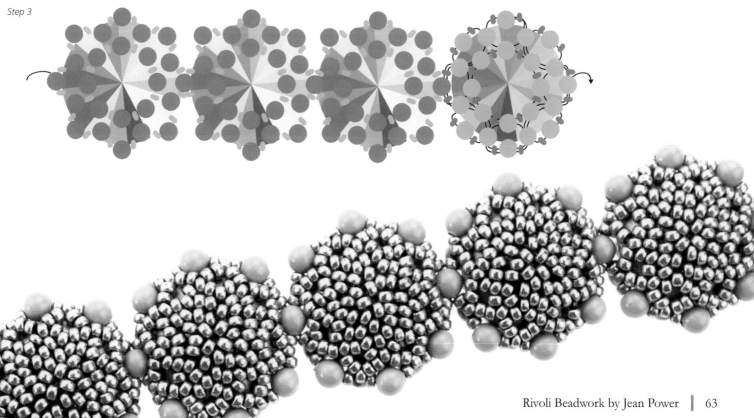

STEP 4

Attaching the clasp.
You can adjust how you attach your clasp depending on what you're using, but the method I used was:
At one end of your bezel weave to exit a Pearl on the outer edge either side of the Pearl opposite the last one shared with the previous bezel. Make sure you're pointing towards the Pearl opposite the shared one.
Pick up 11 x S15 beads (or as many as needed, the diagram shows more) and thread through a loop on your clasp.
Thread into the Pearl 2 on the outer edge 2 along from where you were.
Weave through this thread-path multiple times to secure and then repeat on the other end of the bracelet.

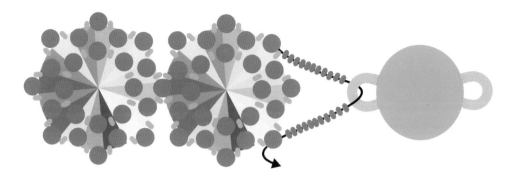

Step 4

Variations

- You can use any of the **RAW Pearls Bezel** variations but you may need to adjust the embellishment where the bezels meet

- You could also add the Outer Edge Embellishment from Step 5 of the **Jo Ellen Pendant** to your bezels. You can either leave off the adding beads bridging between the bezels or experiment with what you use to keep the bracelet flexible

- Also look at the **RAW Pearls Scarf Ring** for other variation ideas

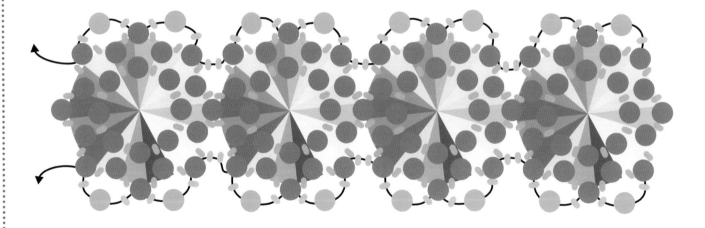

RAW Pearls Scarf Ring

This scarf ring is the perfect way to dress up a plain scarf or outfit and add a bit of sparkle at the same time!

Materials
- 4 x 14mm Rivolis
- 3g of size 15 Miyuki seed beads - your S15 beads
- 92 x 3mm Swarovski Round Pearls #5810 - your P beads

I used
- Rivolis: Fuschia, Blush Rose, Crystal Rose Gold & Amethyst
- Seed beads: Miyuki #4221
- Pearls: Crystal Iridescent Dark Blue

Techniques
- RAW Pearls Bezel - Original Version, Page 46
- Grown From Pearls, Page 54
- Grown From Seeds, Page 55
- Right-Angle Weave
- Peyote Stitch

THE STEPS...
STEP 1
The First Bezel.
Bezel a Rivoli using Steps 1-11 of **The RAW Pearls Bezel - Original Version**.

STEP 2
The Second Bezel.
Weave to exit any P in the outer edge and using the **Grown From Pearls** OR the **Grown from Seeds** method add a 2nd bezel to the 1st making sure it shares just 1 Pearl. This 2nd one can be added to any of the Pearls in the 1st bezel.

STEP 3
The Third Bezel.
Add 1 more bezel using the **Grown From Pearls** OR the **Grown from Seeds** method making sure that it begins from the Pearl directly opposite the one shared with the previous bezel and only shares 1 pearl.

STEP 4
The Fourth Bezel.
Add in a new Bezel using the **Grown from Seeds** method and make sure it is joined to both the 1st and 3rd bezels and sits evenly between them.

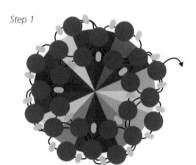

As the components in this scarf ring use the **Grown from Seeds** *method of RAW Pearls, the entire back of the Rivolis won't be covered*

Step 1

Step 2

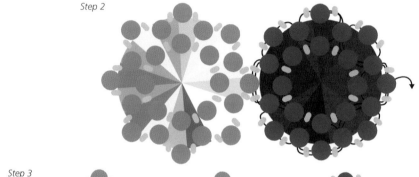

Step 3

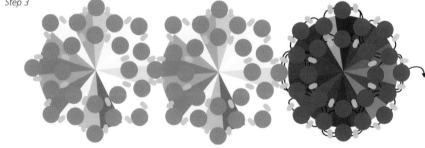

Step 4

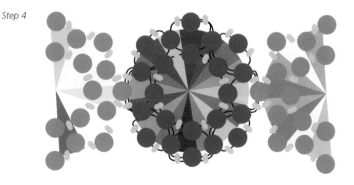

TOP TIP
You have to use the **Grown from Seeds** *method to add in the last Rivoli bezel but you can choose to use this one, or the* **Grown from Pearls** *method, for the others*

Variations

- You can use any of the **RAW Pearls Bezel** variations, but you may need to adjust the embellishment where the bezels meet each other or add more space between the bezels

- You can add 1 or 2 more Rivolis for a larger Scarf Ring or even more than that to turn it into a bangle

- You can add the Outer Edge Embellishment from Step 5 of the **Jo Ellen Pendant** to your bezels. You may need to experiment with what you use to bridge between the bezels

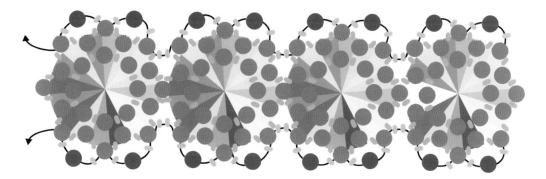

- Why not experiment with adding drops or swags of beads to the bottom edge of your Scarf Ring for extra pizzazz? You can do this instead of the Outer Edge Embellishment suggested above or in combination with it

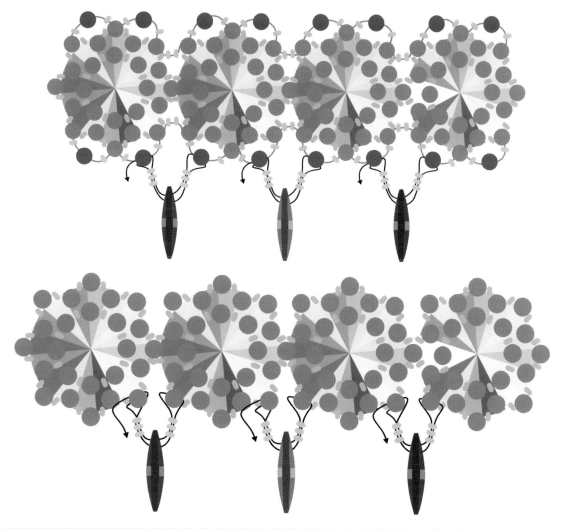

Jo Ellen Pendant

This pendant is formed of multiple bezelled Rivolis with each one growing directly from a previous one in a circle before extra embellishment is added

Materials
- 8 x 14mm Rivolis
- 5g of size 15 Miyuki seed beads - your S15 beads
- 216 x 3mm Swarovski Round Pearls #5810 - your P beads

I used
- Rivolis: Crystal Paradise Shine
- Seed beads: Miyuki #4202
- Pearls: Crystal Iridescent Purple

Techniques
- RAW Pearls Bezel - Original Version, Page 46
- Grown From Pearls, Page 54
- Right-Angle Weave
- Peyote Stitch

THE STEPS...

STEP 1
The first Bezel.
Bezel a Rivoli using Steps 1-11 of the **Raw Pearls Bezel - Original version.**

STEP 2
The second Bezel.
Weave to exit any P in the outer edge and, using the **Grown From Pearls** method, add a 2nd bezel to the 1st making sure this shares only 1 Pearl. This 2nd one can be added to any of the Pearls in the 1st bezel.

STEP 3
Bezels 3-7.
Decide what will be the inner & outer edges of your circle and continue adding bezels using the **Grown From Pearls** method making sure that each one is now spaced so that there are 4 free Pearls on the outer edge of your circle and 2 free Pearls on the inner edge and that each one only shares 1 Pearl with the previous bezel. Do this until there are 7 bezels joined.

STEP 4
The 8th Bezel.
Add a final bezel making sure to join it to both your 7th and 1st bezels so that there are still 4 free Pearls on the outer edge of your circle and 2 free Pearls on the inner edge.

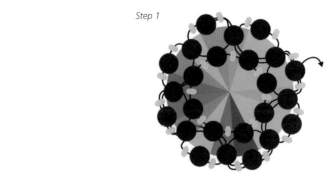
Step 1

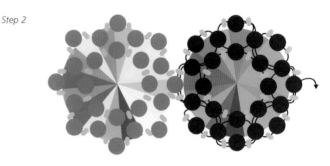
Step 2

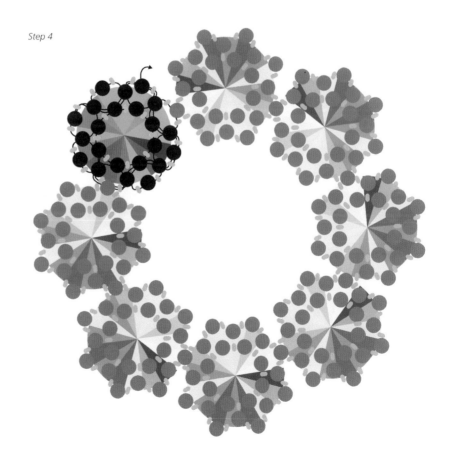
Step 4

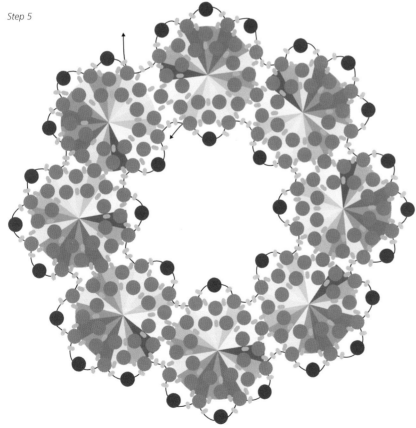

Step 5

STEP 5
The optional Outer Edge Embellishment. Weave to exit any 'unshared' Pearl on the outer edge of any bezel. You will now add a pattern of 3 groups of 1 x S15, 1P and 1 x S15 between 4 of the Pearls on the outer edge and then move to the next Pearl on the next bezel using 2 x S15. Bead this all around the outer edge of the circle (64 x S15, 24P)

The optional Inner Edge Embellishment. Weave to exit either of the 'unshared' Pearls on the inner edge of any bezel facing towards the other appropriate Pearl. Pick up 1 x S15, 1P and 1 x S15 and thread into the next Pearl on the same bezel. Pick up 2 x S15s and thread into the appropriate Pearl on the next bezel. Repeat this pattern of embellishment all around the inner edge (32 x S15, 8P).

STEP 6
Hanging Loop.
Weave to exit any S15 bead sitting near the centre of any of your bezels at the back. Pick up 23 x S15 (you can use more or less if you know what size your stringing materials will be) and thread into any S15 bead at the back of the same bezel towards the bottom/inner edge. Weave back and forth through this thread-path to secure (23 x S15).

Variations

- You can use any of the **RAW Pearls Bezel** variations but you may need to adjust the embellishment where the bezels meet each other

- I have added extra embellishment on the Inner & Outer Edges of the bezels, but this is optional and can be left off

- If you leave off the Outer Embellishment (even just on one bezel) you can add a drop bead or pendant to the outer edge on the lowest bezel, or even inside the pendant for a different look

Josephine Pendant

This 3D Ball Pendant is made up of 6 bezelled Rivolis, each one connected to 4 others. It can be strung on a fine chain or cord through the spaces where 3 Rivolis intersect

Materials
- 6 x 14mm Rivolis
- 4g of size 15 Miyuki seed beads - your S15 beads
- 132 x 3mm Swarovski Round Pearls #5810 - your P beads

I used
- Rivolis: Aquamarine
- Seed beads: Miyuki #4221
- Pearls: Crystal Iridescent Dark Blue

Techniques
- RAW Pearls Bezel - Original Version, Page 46
- Grown From Pearls, Page 54
- Grown From Seeds, Page 55
- Right-Angle Weave
- Peyote Stitch

THE STEPS...

STEP 1
Bezels 1-4.
Bead Steps 1-4 of **RAW Pearls Scarf Ring** to join your first 4 Rivolis into a circle.

STEP 2
Bezel 5.
Using the **Grown from Seeds** method add a 5th Rivoli bezel on one edge of your circle making sure It shares 1 Pearl with each of the 4 bezels already there.

STEP 3
Bezel 6.
Using the **Grown from Seeds** method add a 6th Rivoli bezel on the other edge of your circle making sure It shares 1 Pearl with each of the 4 bezels already there.

> **TOP TIP**
> *If you know what you're going to string the Ball Pendant on you can add it in before you add your last bezels which is easier to do than threading it through the gaps later*

> **TOP TIP**
> *You have to use the **Grown from Seeds** method to add in at least 3 of the Rivolis, but you can choose to use this one, or the **Grown from Pearls** method, for the others*

Daphne Pendant

This pendant is formed of a large crystal, extra embellishment, and a crystal drop added for extra sparkle

Materials
- 1 x 27mm Swarovski Crown Stone #1201
- 4g of size 15 Miyuki seed beads - S15s
- 48 x 3mm Swarovski Round Pearls #5810 - your P beads
- 1 x 32mm Swarovski Ellipse Drop Pendant #6470 or similar

I used
- Crown Stone: Golden Chestnut
- Seed beads: Miyuki #4203
- Pearls: Dark Lapis
- Drop Pendant: Red Magma

Techniques
- RAW Pearls - Larger Bezel, Page 50
- Right-Angle Weave
- Peyote Stitch

THE STEPS...
STEP 1
The Bezel.
Using the **Raw Pearls Larger Bezel** principle bezel your 27mm Crystal and cover the back. Finish by exiting any S15 on the inner edge at the front of your bezel.

THE EMBELLISHMENT...
This is made by adding S15 loops (where the first and last bead of each loop is shared with another loop) and then weaving through the loops again, missing out the central bead, which makes it 'pop' out.

STEP 2
Pick up 5 x S15 and thread into the next S15 along in the Bezel.
Thread back through the last S15, pick up 4 x S15 and thread into the next S15 in the bezel. Repeat from * to * all around the inner edge finishing by picking up just 3 x S15s and thread into the first one picked up in this step. Step-Up to exit the 2nd S15 picked up (64 x S15).

STEP 3
Missing the central S15 in each loop from Step 2 weave through the others.

STEP 4
Adding the Drop.
There are different ways you can attach the Drop but the method I used was:
Exiting any P on the outer edge of the bezel, pick up 14 x S15 and the Drop Pendant, thread into the next P on the outer edge.

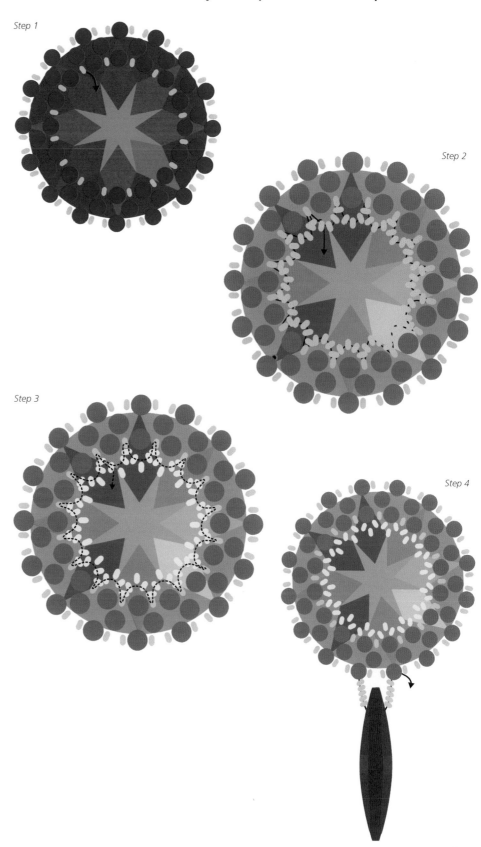

Step 1

Step 2

Step 3

Step 4

STEP 5

Hanging Loop.
Weave to exit any S15 bead sitting near the centre of your bezel at the back. Pick up 23 x S15 (you can use more or less if you know what size your stringing materials will be) and thread into any S15 bead at the back of the bezel towards the top/ outer edge. Weave back and forth through this thread-path to secure (23 x S15).

Variations

- You can use any of the **RAW Pearls Bezel** variations to add a different look

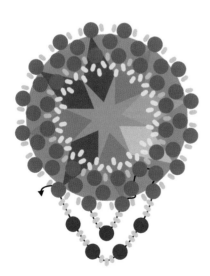

- Instead of a Drop Pendant you could add swags of S15s and Pearls to the bottom of your piece

- You could also add the Outer Edge Embellishment from Step 5 of the **Jo Ellen Pendant** to your bezel. You may need to experiment with the exact beads you pick up as you do this

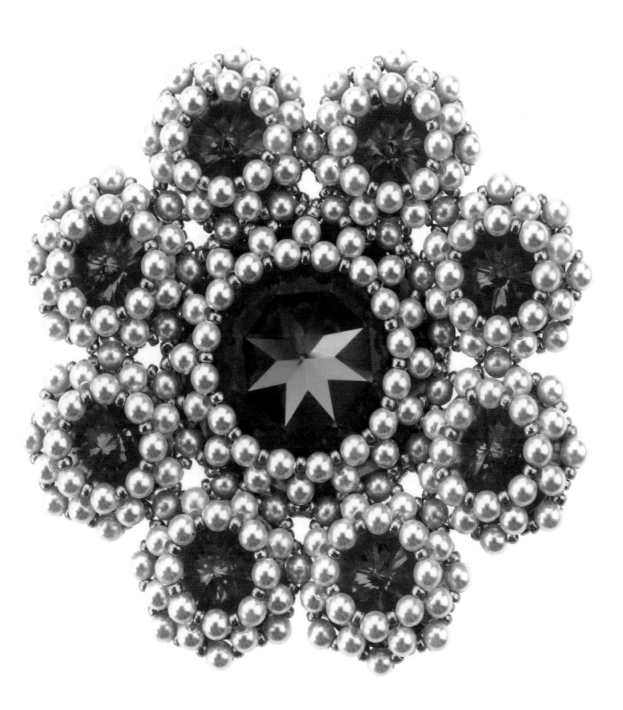

Marlene Pendant

This brooch/ pendant is formed of a large focal crystal surrounded by 8 Rivolis all bezelled using the RAW Pearls technique to create a striking piece of beadwork

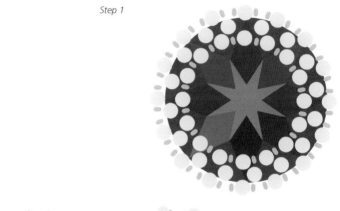

Step 1

Materials
- 8 x 14mm Rivolis
- 1 x 27mm Swarovski Crown Stone #1201
- 8g of size 15 Miyuki seed beads - your S15 beads
- 216 x 3mm Swarovski Round Pearls #5810 - your P beads

I used
- Rivolis: Rose
- Crown Stone: Rose
- Seed beads: Miyuki #4203
- Pearls: Crystal Cream Rose

Techniques
- RAW Pearls Bezel - Original Version, Page 46
- RAW Pearls - Making a Larger Bezel, Page 50
- Grown From Pearls, Page 54
- Right-Angle Weave
- Peyote Stitch

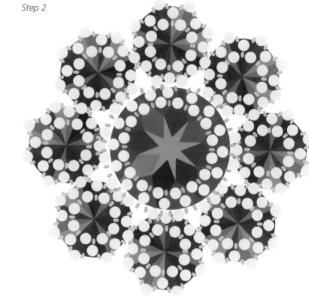

Step 2

THE STEPS...
STEP 1
The Central Bezel.
Using Steps 1-15 of **Making a Larger RAW Pearl Bezel** make a bezel around your Crown Stone.

STEP 2
The Rivolis
Using **Grown from Pearls** bead 8 x 14mm Rivoli bezels around the central bezel, each one sharing 2 Pearls with the central bezel and 1 Pearl with each Rivoli bezel on each side of it.

STEP 3
Hanging Loop.
Weave to exit any S15 sitting near the centre of any of your 14mm Rivoli bezels at the back. Pick up 23 x S15 (you can use more or less if you know what size your stringing materials will be) and thread into any S15 bead at the back of the same bezel towards the bottom/ inner edge. Weave back and forth through this thread-path to secure (23 x S15).

Step 3

Variations

- You can use any of the **RAW Pearls Bezel** variations but may need to adjust the embellishment where bezels meet

- You don't need to add Rivoli bezels all the way around your central bezel. Instead you can just add 4 alternately spaced ones, or 3 or 5 just at the top to change the shape (with or without a Pendant Drop for extra pizzazz)

- You could also add the Outer Edge Embellishment from Step 5 of the **Jo Ellen Pendant** to your Rivoli bezels. You may need to experiment with the exact beads you pick up as you do this

Laura Necklace

Combine a large bezelled crystal with 2 Rivolis and oodles of Pearls for a classic and timeless necklace

Materials
- 2 x 14mm Rivolis
- 1 x 27mm Swarovski Crown Stone #1201
- 9g of size 15 Miyuki seed beads - S15s
- Approximately 286 x 3mm Swarovski Round Pearls #5810 - your P beads

I used
- Rivolis & Crown Stone: Crystal
- Seed beads: Miyuki #4201
- Pearls: Crystal Cream Rose

Techniques
- RAW Pearls Bezel - Original Version, Page 46
- RAW Pearls - Making a Larger Bezel, Page 50
- Grown From Pearls, Page 54
- Right-Angle Weave
- Peyote Stitch

THE STEPS...

STEP 1
The Central Bezel.
Using Steps 1-15 of **Beading a Larger RAW Pearl Bezel** make a bezel around your large crystal.

STEP 2
Using **Grown from Pearls** bead 2 x 14mm Rivoli bezels each one sharing 1 single Pearl with the central bezel and leaving 3 outer edge Pearls on the central bezel empty between them.

STEP 3
Beading the Toggle.
Using S15s bead a piece of Odd-Count Peyote Stitch 15 beads wide and 10 rows tall. Bring the edges together to zip the work into a tube. Weave to exit one end of the tube and pick up 1 x P and 1 x S15. Missing the S15, thread back through the P and thread to exit the other end of the tube. Pick up 1 x P and 1 x S15. Missing the S15, thread back through the P and weave back and forth through the same thread-path to secure. Weave away the thread.

ADDING THE BEADED CHAIN...
The chain used for the rest of the necklace is made up of units of RAW using S15s and Pearls. You'll weave around each unit a couple of times to make the central S15 in each corner pop out. You'll also pick up 1 extra S15 in each unit on the outer edge to give your chain a gentle curve.

STEP 4
On either of your 14mm Rivoli bezels weave to exit the Pearl on the outer edge which is directly opposite the one shared with the large crystal bezel. Make sure you do this

so you are exiting the Pearl facing away from the other Rivoli bezel. Pick up 3 x S15, 1P, 2 x S15, 1P, 3 x S15, 1P, 3 x S15, 1P, 1 x S15, 1P and 3 x S15s. Circle through the Pearl you were exiting.

STEP 5
Weave all around the beads picked up in the last step BUT, whenever you get to a group of 3 x S15, ignore the central one and only thread through the other 2. Pull tight and this will make the central S15 pop out. Finish by weaving to exit the Pearl opposite the one shared with the central bezel ready to continue.

STEP 6
Add 1 more unit of RAW but this time pick up: 3 x S15, 1P, 1 x S15, 1P, 3 x S15, 1P, 3 x S15, 1P, 2 x S15, 1P and 3 x S15. Continue adding RAW units, alternating the 2 different groups of beads that you've picked up so far and making sure that the single S15 always sits on the inner edge of the chain. After you add each circle weave through again to make the corner S15s pop out. Stop when this side of the chain is as long as desired.

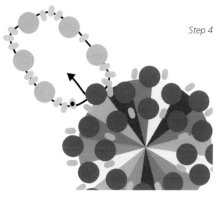
Step 4

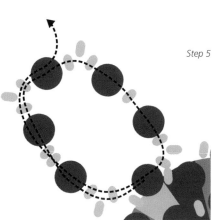
Step 5

Step 6

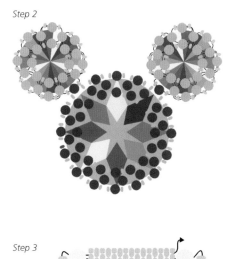
Step 2

Step 3

STEP 7

Repeat Steps 4-6 for the other half of your chain beginning on your other 14mm Rivoli bezel. Make sure to add the single S15 on the inner edge of the chain. When this side is as long as desired, instead of picking up the central Pearl on your last RAW unit, thread into your toggle to secure it to your chain to finish the fastening.

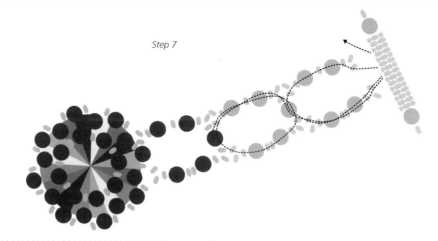

Step 7

Variations

- Why not add an extra Rivoli bezel to the bottom of your large crystal bezel?

- To add extra Pearls, why not add use the principle of the Outer Edge Embellishment from Step 5 of the **Jo Ellen Pendant** to your bezels. You may need to experiment with the exact beads you use as you do this

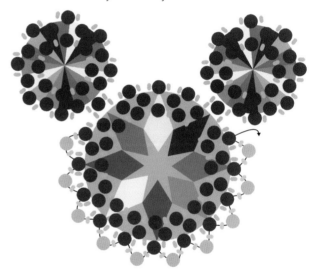

- You could add a Drop or swag of S15s and Pearls to the bottom of your central bezel

Herringbone Pearls
Herringbone Stitch & Pearls unite in these quick Rivoli bezels

Materials
Each Herringbone Pearl uses:
- 1 x 14mm Rivoli
- 1g of size 15 Miyuki seed beads - S15s
- 1g size 11 cylinder beads - C beads
- 8 x 3mm Swarovski Round Pearls #5810 - your P beads

I used
- Rivolis: Swarovski; Light Turquoise, Siam & Light Rose. Matubo; Sky Blue Pearl, Coral & Pink Opal
- Seed beads: Miyuki #4202
- Cylinder beads: DB1153
- Pearls: Red Coral, Crystal Turquoise & Crystal Coral

Techniques
- RAW Pearls - The Back, Page 48
- Herringbone Stitch

THE STEPS...

STEP 1
First Unit – First Step.
Pick up 1 x C, 1 Pearl and 4 x C. Circle through the 2nd & 3rd C beads in the group of 4 (5 x C and 1 x P).

STEP 2
First Unit – Second Step.
Pick up 2 x C and using Herringbone Stitch add them (threading into the 4th C bead added in the group of 4 in Step 1) and then circle through 1 more C bead (the 2nd of the group of 4 added in Step 1) (2 x C).

STEP 3
Units 2-8.
Repeat Steps 1-2 seven more times to add a total of 8 units. Finish by circling through 1C, 1P and 4 x C to exit the first C bead added in Step 2 (49 x C and 7 x P).

STEP 4
Second Round.
You'll now change direction. Using Herringbone Stitch, add 1 x C on top of each of the 8 Herringbone Units in your circle, threading down and up 2C in each unit. As you move between each unit add 1 x S15. As you bead this round, your Herringbone Units will pull in tighter and your Pearls will move to form an outer circle (8 x C and 8 x S15).

STEP 5
Third Round.
You now need to weave around just threading through the top 3 C beads in each unit and moving from unit to unit with no beads. This is done to hold your Rivoli in securely. At the end, finish by weaving to exit any C bead from Step 1 or 3 which sits either side of a Pearl facing towards the next unit (no beads added this step).

STEP 6
Fourth Round.
Pick up 1C and thread through the next C, Pearl and C from Step 1 or 3. Repeat seven more times to complete this round. finishing by exiting the first C added (8 x C).

STEP 7
The Back.
Bead Steps 6-10 of **RAW Pearls** (Rounds 2-7 of the back) using S15 beads to cover the back of your bezel.

Step 1

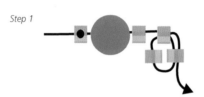

Step 3

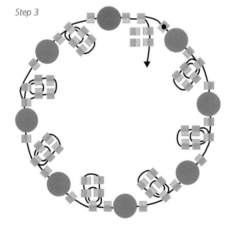

Step 5

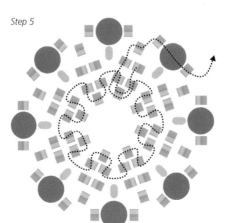

Step 2

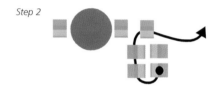

Step 4

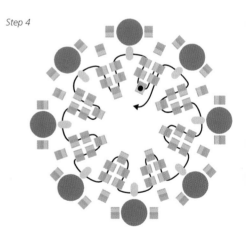

Step 6

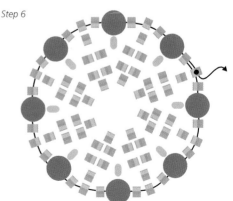

Variations

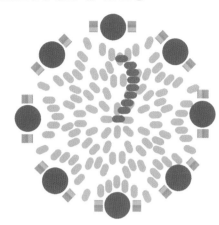

- Hanging Loop at back;
Weave to exit any S15 bead at the back of your bezel near the centre. Pick up 7-15 x S15 (you can use more or less if you know what size your stringing material will be) and thread into any S15 bead at the back of the same bezel towards the top edge. Weave back and forth through this thread-path to secure

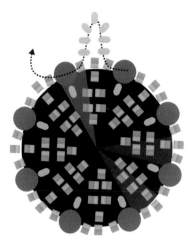

- Hanging Loop on outer edge;
Weave to exit any C bead either side of a Pearl on the outer edge. Pick up as many S15 or C beads as desired and then thread into the next C bead on the outer edge

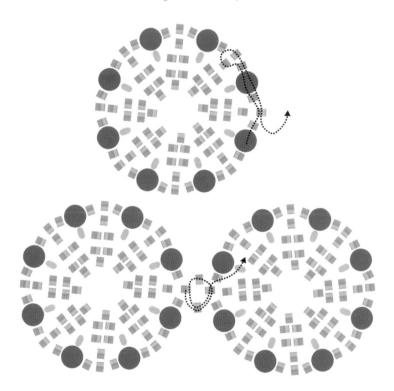

- Individual Herringbone Pearls can be linked to each other to form bracelets, bangles, necklace centrepieces or scarf rings. A quick & easy way to join them is to use Peyote Stitch to add in a C bead along an edge – there is the perfect space to do this between 2 C beads between 2 Pearls. You can then add a single unit of Right-Angle Weave to join two bezels or join them using tabs as shown on the **Star Flower** variation (Page 34)

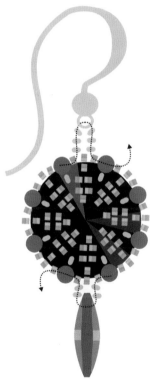

- Herringbone Pearls can be turned into adorned pendants or earrings by adding a drop along a bottom edge and using S15 beads to add a hanging loop or to attach to an earring finding

Pearl Buds

From one beginning, many buds form...

These pieces all begin from a Basic Rivoli Bezel and then, using the same principle, they all grow in different directions.

The 9 different bezels I show here begin from either a 9 Pearl Base (with 9 separate Pearl Buds) or an 18 Pearl Base (this has 18 Pearl Buds all of which are joined together)

Materials
The full necklace, which has 1 of each style of Pearl Buds bezel, and is 21 inches/ 53cm long uses:
- 9 x 14mm Rivolis
- 10g of size 15 Miyuki seed beads - S15 beads
- 6g of size 11 Cylinder beads - C beads
- 139 x 3mm Swarovski Round Pearls #5810 - P beads

I used
- Rivolis: Ochre DeLite
- Seed beads: Miyuki #4203
- Cylinder beads: DB2043
- Pearls: Lapis

Techniques
- Stitch-In-The-Ditch, Page 11
- Basic Bezelling Technique, Page 12
- Peyote Stitch

18 Pearl Base

STEP 1
Bezelling the Rivoli
Using the **Basic Bezelling instructions** bezel a 14mm Rivoli and weave to exit any of the C beads in the central round.

STEP 2
Adding the first Pearl
Pick up 3 x S15, 1 x P and 3 x S15. Circle through the C you were exiting on the bezel base and then weave to exit the next C on the central round (6 x S15, 1P).

> **TOP TIP**
> *As you add subsequent Pearls your seed beads will overlap each other and the Pearls – just let this happen and the seeds come to the front*

STEP 3
Adding Pearl 2
Pick up 3 x S15 and 1P. Thread through the 3rd and 2nd S15 picked up in Step 2 to link the 2 Buds and then pick up 1 x S15 and circle through the C you were exiting and weave to exit the next C on the central round (4 x S15, 1P).

STEP 4
Adding Pearls 3-17
Repeat Step 3 fifteen more times to add a total of 17 Pearl Buds (60 x S15 and 15 x P).

STEP 5
Adding the 18th Pearl Bud
Pick up 1 x S15 and thread through the 5th and 4th S15 picked up in Step 2. Pick up 1 x P and thread through the 3rd and 2nd S15s on the last Pearl Bud in Step 4. Pick up 1 x S15 and circle through the C you were exiting on the bezel base (2 x S15, 1 x P).

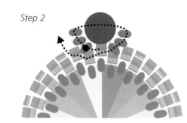
Step 2

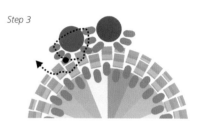
Step 3

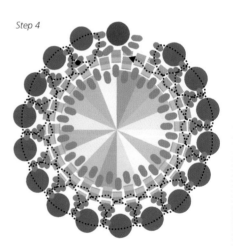
Step 4

Step 5

9 Pearl Base

STEP 1
Bezelling the Rivoli.
Using the **Basic Bezelling Technique** bezel a 14mm Rivoli and weave to exit any of the C beads in the central round.

STEP 2
Adding Pearls.
Pick up 3 x S15, 1 x P and 3 x S15. Circle through the C you were exiting on the bezel base and then weave to exit the next C 2 beads along on the central round from the one you were exiting (6 x S15, 1 x P).

STEP 3
Repeat Step 2 eight more times to add a total of 9 Pearls (48 x S15, 8 P).

Step 2

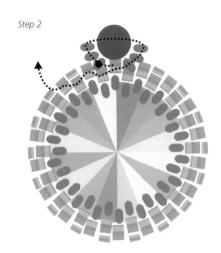

Step 3

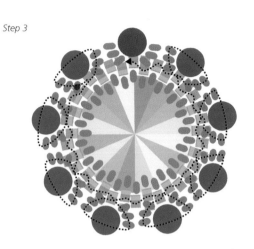

BASIC 9 PEARL BUD

These are beaded by using Steps 1-3 of the **9 Pearl Base**

BASIC 18 PEARL BUD

These are beaded using Steps 1-5 of the **18 Pearl Base**

SIMPLE STRANDS

STEP 1
Getting started
Bead Steps 1-5 of **18 Pearl Base** and then Step-Up to exit the first 3 x S15s picked up.

STEP 2
Pick up 2-3 x S15s (I alternated between picking up 3 x S15s and 2 x S15s on mine) and missing the last one thread down the other beads picked up and then through your work to exit the next 3 x S15s on the other side of the next Pearl. Repeat adding these small strands until each space is filled (2-3 x S15 per Pearl).

Step 2

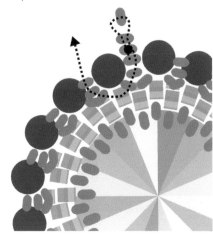

ENCLOSED 9 PEARL BUDS

Step 1

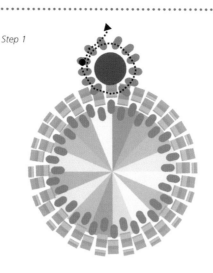

Step 2

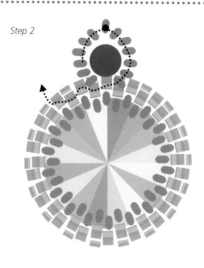

STEP 1
Beginning and enclosing the Pearl.
Bead Steps 1-2 of **9 Pearl Base** but, at the end, instead of weaving to exit the next C bead, Step-Up to exit the first 3 x S15s picked up. Pick up 6 x S15 and circle through the next 3 x S15, the C on the base, the original 3 x S15s and the first 3 new S15s (6 x S15).

STEP 2
Adding a Picot.
Pick up 1 x S15 and circle through the next 6 x S15s and the C you were exiting. Weave to exit the C bead 2 beads along on the bezel base to add another Enclosed Pearl Bud (1 x S15).

SIMPLE FRAMES

Step 2

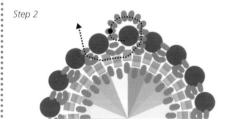

Step 3

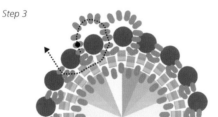

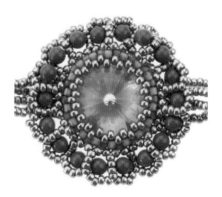

STEP 1
Getting started.
Bead Steps 1-5 of **18 Pearl Base** and then Step-Up to exit the first 3 x S15s picked up.

STEP 2
Framing the first Pearl Bud.
Pick up 8 x S15 and circle through the next 3 x S15, the C on the base and weave to exit the first 3 x S15s picked up the other side of the next Pearl (8 x S15).

Step 4

STEP 3
Framing the 2nd-17th Pearl Bud.
Pick up 6 x S15 and thread down the first 2 x S15 picked up to frame the previous Pearl and then the S15s around this pearl. Weave through your work to again Step-Up to exit the first 3 x S15 on the next Pearl. Repeat this process fifteen more times to frame a total of 17 Pearls (96 x S15).

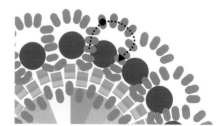

STEP 4
Framing the 18th Pearl Bud
The last Pearl Bud needs just 4 x S15s added to frame it. To add these you first need to Step-Up to exit the last 2 x S15s which frame the first Pearl. Then pick up 4 x S15s and thread through the first 2 x S15s, framing the 17th Pearl (4 x S15).

PICOT FRAMES

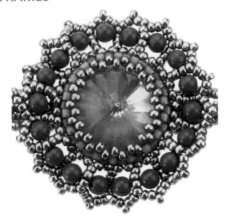

STEP 1
Getting started. Bead Steps 1- 4 of 'Simple Frames'.

STEP 2
Adding the Picots.
Weave to exit the first 2 S15s in any group of 4 unshared above a Pearl. Pick up 1 x S15 and thread through the next 2 x S15s in the 4 and the first two in the next group of 4 above a Pearl. Repeat this to add a Picot above each Pearl (18 x S15).

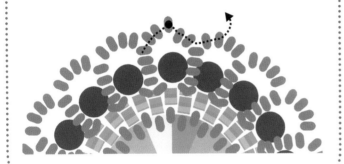

JOINING POINTS

The bezel in the photo also has the Extra Adornment as mentioned below

STEP 1
Adding the joins.
Bead a Basic **9 Pearl Base** and then Step-Up to exit the first 3 x S15s picked up. Pick up 3 x S15s and, missing the last 1, thread down 1. Pick up 1 x S15 and thread down the next 3 x S15s by the next Pearl and then weave to exit the 3 x S15s on the other side. Repeat to add 9 joins in total (4 x S15 per join).

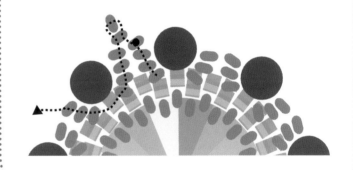

You can add extra Pearls to any of your **9 Pearl Base** variations by following these simple steps. You can see how they look on my **Joining Points** variation

STEP 1
Laying in the base beads
As you add each Pearl Bud and move between the groups of 3 x S15s you can pick up 1 x S15 so it sits underneath your Pearl.

STEP 2
Then later on you can weave between these extra beads adding in 1 x S15, 1P and 1 x S15 until each space is filled.

Extra Adornment

Step 1

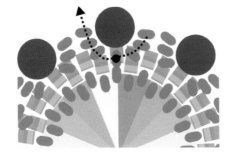

Step 2

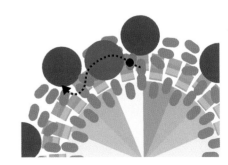

CROWNS

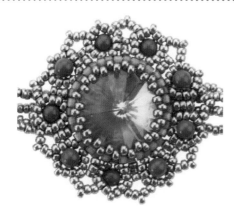

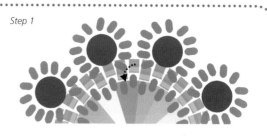

STEP 1

Preparing.

Bead the principle of Step 1 of the **Enclosed 9 Pearl Buds** (to add 6 x S15s above each Bud) all around the Rivoli. Weave through to exit any C bead in the central round of the bezel base which does not have a Pearl Bud on it.

TOP TIP

As you add all the seed beads they may overlap each other and the previous ones - just let this happen and the new seeds come to the front

Step 2

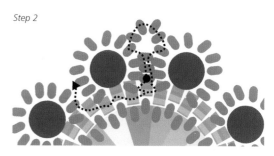

STEP 2

Pick up 3 x S15 and thread up the 4th S15 up from where you are which enclose either of the nearest Pearls. Pick up 4 x S15 and thread down the 4th S15 from the bezel base by the other Pearl nearest you. Thread down the 3 new seeds, circle through the C you were exiting, and move onto the next C on the base without a Pearl above it. Repeat this all around your Rivoli (7 x S15 per Pearl).

Step 3

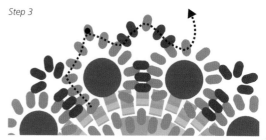

STEP 3

Adding the Picots.

Weave to exit the 6th seed bead originally surrounding any Pearl.

*Pick up 1 x S15 and thread through 1 of the seeds around the Pearl.

Thread into the first 2 x S15s in the next 4-bead loop added in the last step.

Pick up 1 x S15 and thread through the other 2 x S15s added in the last step and then thread into the 6th S15 above the next Pearl*.

Repeat from * to * eight more times to finish the round (18 x S15).

Step 1

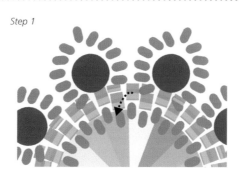

Step 2

ADORNED CROWNS

STEP 1

Bead Steps 1-2 of the **Enclosed 9 Pearl Buds** all around the Rivoli. Weave through to exit any C bead in the central round of the bezel base which does not have a Pearl Bud on it.

STEP 2

Pick up 3 x S15 and thread up the 4th S15 up from where you are which encloses either of the nearest Pearls. Pick up 1 x S15, 1P, and 3 x S15. Missing the last 3 S15s, thread back down the Pearl and pick up 1 x S15. Thread down the 4th S15 from the bezel base by the other Pearl nearest you. Thread down the 3 new seeds, circle through the C you were exiting, and move onto the next C on the base without a Pearl above it. Repeat this all around your Rivoli (8 x S15 and 1P per Pearl).

Making the necklace
Unite your Pearl Buds for a striking necklace...

My necklace uses 9 bezelled Rivolis (one of each of the Pearl Bud variations), all joined together with 10 beaded links and then finished with a Toggle Clasp

Making & Using Beaded Links

MAKING LINKS
STEP 1
Rounds 1-5. Pick up 36 x S15 and thread through the first 2 to join into a circle. Using Peyote Stitch and S15s add 3 more rounds with 18 x S15 in each (90 x S15).

STEP 2
Rounds 6-7. Using Peyote Stitch and C beads add 2 rounds with 18 beads in each (36 x C).

STEP 3
Return to your tail or weave to exit any S15 bead in the first round.

STEP 4
Round 8. Using C beads add 1 round (18 x C).

STEP 5
Zip the edges of your beadwork together to securely join them. As you do this the C beads added in Round 7 will pull towards this side of your work and end up sitting along the central outer edge of your ring. Weave away your threads to finish.

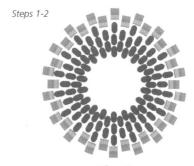

Steps 1-2

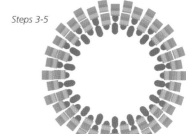

Steps 3-5

USING LINKS
I linked my necklace together with loops of 36 x S15 beads. I added 4 loops to each Rivoli in total (2 at each side) but feel free to experiment with that and how many beads are in the loops

STEP 1
Weave to exit any C bead in the last round of C beads at the back of a bezel. Pick up as many S15s as desired (I used 36) and thread through your Beaded Link. Then circle back through the C you were exiting in the bezel.

STEP 2
Weave to exit the next C in the same round of the bezel and pick up the same number of S15 beads again. Circle through your Beaded Link as before BUT you must make sure you mirror your previous line of S15s so the piece looks coordinated. So, if the 'bottom strand' of the first loop lay under the Beaded Link (as in the diagrams), this time the 'top strand' of the new loop must lay under the Beaded Link.

STEP 3
Circle through your C bead in the bezel base and then weave to exit the 8th C bead along to repeat this at the other side of the Rivoli if needed.

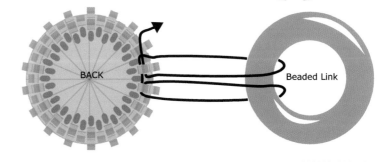

TOP TIP
You want the different colours 'strands' in the diagram below to match whether they lay on top of or underneath the Beaded Link

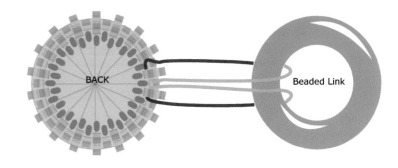

The Toggle Clasp

The necklace can be finished with a Toggle Clasp which threads into a Beaded Link on each end. I like to make multiple Toggles, each separated with a different number of S15s between the Toggle ends, so that I can wear my finished necklace at different lengths as desired

STEP 1
Beading the Toggle Ends.
Using S beads, and Odd-Count Peyote Stitch, bead a piece of beadwork 17 beads wide and 8 rows tall.

STEP 2
Bring the edges together to zip the work into a tube.

STEP 3
Weave to exit one end of the tube and pick up 1 x Pearl and 1 x S15. Missing the S15, thread back through the Pearl and thread to exit the other end of the tube.

STEP 4
Pick up 1 x Pearl and 1 x S15. Missing the S, thread back through the Pearl and weave back and forth through the same thread-path to secure.

STEP 5
Weave away the thread and repeat to make a second Toggle End but keep the thread on this new one (70 x S15 and 2P for each Toggle).

STEP 6
Finishing the Toggle Clasp.
The Toggles now need to be joined together with a strand of S beads. Weave the thread exiting the second Toggle to the middle of its length so you exit any of the 4 central beads along the width. Pick up as many S beads as desired (I used 18 on my shortest one). Thread into a matching bead on the middle of the side of your other Toggle. Exit the bead and then thread back up the strand of beads. Thread back into your first Toggle where you exited (threading into the bead hole on the other side than you exited it) and weave back and forth through the thread-path to secure and then finish your thread.

Steps 1-4

Step 6

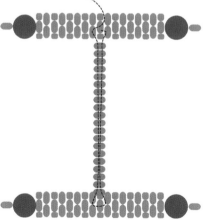

Geometric

Taking your Rivoli beadwork in
a geometric direction can have
some amazing results...

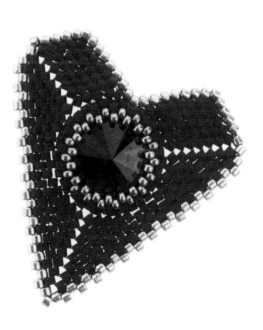

Geometric Basics

Learn all the basic techniques needed for the geometric projects in this book...

Herringbone Increase

A Herringbone Increase can be added into any space where you want to increase your beadwork.

It is beaded by using 2 beads in a space instead of 1, and by threading into the next bead in the previous row or rounds, and not missing one.

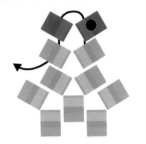

In the next round, if you are still increasing, you exit the first bead of the previous pair, pick up 2 beads and thread into the second bead of the pair

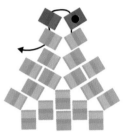

Beading a Triangle

STEP 1
Round 1 – Pick up 3 beads. Join them into a circle by circling through the first one again.

STEP 2
Round 2 – An Increasing Round. Bead this using a total of 6 beads (added in 3 pairs) by adding a **Herringbone Increase** (see above) into each gap between the beads in Round 1. This forms the corners of your triangle.

STEP 3
Round 3 – An Increasing Round. Bead a round with 2 beads on top of 2 (A **Herringbone Increase**) in the corners and 1 bead everywhere else (these are the side spaces and you begin with just 1 each side and these increase by 1 each side for each extra Increasing Round you bead). This round uses 9 beads.

STEP 4
Round 4 onwards - Continue beading Increasing Rounds with 2 beads on top of 2 (a **Herringbone Increase**) in the corners and 1 bead everywhere else/ the side spaces. You'll find that each extra round you bead needs 3 extra beads:
- Round 4 uses 12 beads
- Round 5 would use 15 beads
- Round 6 would use 18 beads

STEP 5
Point Round - Add a round with just 1 bead in every space.

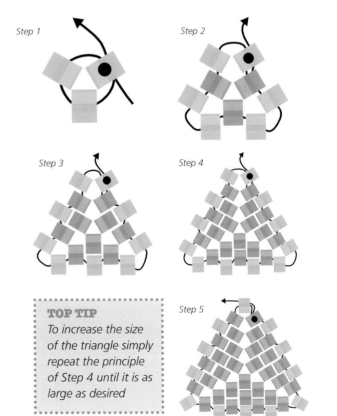

Step 1

Step 2

Step 3

Step 4

Step 5

TOP TIP
To increase the size of the triangle simply repeat the principle of Step 4 until it is as large as desired

Zipping & Joining Triangles

PREPARING TO ZIP

Before you can zip pieces together, they need to be the correct size and shape. Even though it seems wrong you don't want each piece to be the same size (as in this diagram) as then the 'teeth' beads will meet face on rather than slotting together.

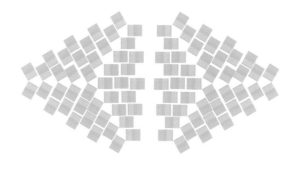

Instead you want to add a Point Round (see Step 5 on previous page) to one piece, which will let them unite as desired.

HOW TO ZIP

When you are adding the Point Round to your next Triangle, weave between your two Triangles, threading through the beads in the Point Round of the first Triangle 'adding' the beads to the 2nd Triangle.

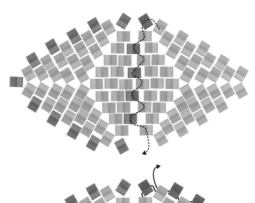

Then fill in the rest of the Point Round beads on the 2nd Triangle to finish it and add the necessary beads for any subsequent Triangles to zip to

Counting Beads

When I state how many beads are on an edge, I count them by including all of the beads along one side, including one from each **Herringbone Increase** (see previous page) in each corner, as shown

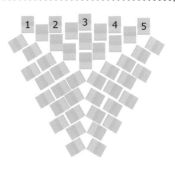

Playing With Triangles

There are many ways to mix-and-match triangles in your work and here are some ideas to get you started...

BRACELETS

The **Slanted Bracelet** could be beaded using **Full Rivoli Triangles,** or **Triangle Bezels** or even just 'plain' triangles beaded using the **Beading a Triangle** instructions. You can even make it more dimensional by using the layering principle used in the **Layered Triangle Pendant** for a different look.

You also don't need to stick to using just one type of triangle in your work...

Imagine a bracelet mixing a few different types for a unique look...

NECKLACES

I have included 2 necklace designs in this chapter but there are so many ways that triangles can be joined so there is endless scope for playing with ideas.

A large, or small, necklace, can be created using **Open Rivoli Triangles, Full Rivoli Triangles,** or **Triangle Bezels** or even just 'plain' triangles made with the **Beading a Triangle** instructions. They can also be made with the dimensionality used in the **Layered Triangle Pendant**.

Also remember that you never need to stick to using just one type (or size) of triangle in your work...
...imagine a necklace mixing all the different types of triangles contained within these pages for a piece that's uniquely you...

DIFFERENT SIZED TRIANGLES

Triangles don't always need to be the same size to be joined together. Depending on what you're beading you can zip together different sizes to create something new. You just need to make sure you add in any needed **Point Round** (see Step 5 on Page 96) beads as you go

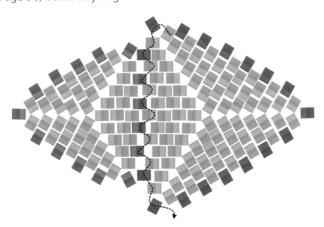

PYRAMIDS

These can be made with any of the triangles described in the book...

PENDANTS

All of the different triangle bezels shown within these pages can be turned into a pendant with either a **Beaded Tab** (Page 20) added to an edge or a **Hanging Loop** (Page 19) added at the back

HEARTS

A Rivoli heart can be made from any triangle that is 12 beads a side so you can use **Full Rivoli Triangles, Open Rivoli Triangles, Triangle Bezels,** or even the principle of a **Layered Triangle Pendant**

BAILS

This chapter has 2 different **Distorted Square** bails used in the projects:

- Distorted Squares with open centres for **Flying Vs**

- Fully beaded Distorted Squares for **Mixed Shape Set** and **Triple Square Pendant**

Either of these bails can be substituted for the other one as desired and they can also be added to any of the bezelled Rivolis in this book...

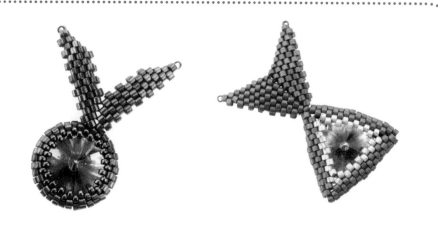

ADDING DEPTH

Both the **Open Rivoli Triangles** and **Full Rivoli Triangles** can have depth added to them so you can join 2 of them back-to-back (see Steps 2-3 of **Double-Sided Bunting** on Page 107 for details on how to do this). You just need to make sure you always add an odd-number of 'plain' rounds of Peyote Stitch (with just 1 bead in each space) to do this

ADDING A BACK

If you've 'added depth' to your rivoli bezel, you can then either zip on another bezel to make a reversible piece (see Step 3 of **Double-Sided Bunting** on Page 107 for details on how to do this) or you can decrease the back to fully cover it (see Steps 3-5 of **Triangle Bezel** for details on how this is beaded)

EARRINGS

Any of the triangles I show in this book could be used to make a pair of earrings. You can play around with different ones making a variation of the **Mixed Shape Earrings** (Page 123) or simply add an earring finding through any corner bead as I did on my **Teardrop Set Earrings** or add 'depth' to any triangle by beading an odd-number of 'plain' Peyote Stitch rounds after the Point Round (See Step 2 of **Double-Sided Bunting**, Page 107 for how this is done) and then decrease the back whilst adding in an earring finding as I did in Steps 4-5 of **Mixed Shape Set Earrings**

THE NEXT STEP

If you want to really experiment with Triangles then you might like to know that:

- 5 triangles make a 'cupped disc' (see the **Full Circle Teardrop** project for an example of how they'll be joined)
- 6 triangles make a flat circle (again see the **Full Circle Teardrop** project for an example of how they'll be joined)
- 20 triangles joined together make a ball (search for 'Icosahedron' for examples...)

Open Rivoli Triangles
Learn how to combine geometry & sparkle with these versatile beaded shapes...

Open Rivoli Triangles grow directly from a Rivoli bezelled using the Basic Bezelling Technique and allow you to adapt your favourite geometric beading projects to contain a bit of extra sparkle & colour

STEP 1
Bezel a 14mm Rivoli using the **Basic Bezelling Technique**. Weave to exit any C bead in the central round of C beads. Pick up 14 x C beads. Count along the same round you're in and go into the 4th bead along (14 x C).

> **TOP TIP**
> *If you had to add more rounds of C beads to your Bezel then you can choose either of the central rounds of C beads to do this extra beading in*

STEP 2
Peyote Stitch a single C bead into each of the next 2 spaces (2 x C).

STEP 3
Repeat Steps 1-2 twice more and then Step-Up to exit the first of the 14 C beads added in Step 1 (32 x C).

STEP 4
Bead 3 single Peyote Stitches, add a **Herringbone Increase** (Page 96), and then lastly 3 more single peyote stitches to turn the loop of beads into a Triangle Point (8 x C).

STEP 5
Bead 3 single Peyote Stitches to take you to the next loop of 14 C beads (3 x C).

STEP 6
Repeat Steps 4-5 twice more to go all the way around your beadwork. Make sure you finish by stepping up to exit the first bead added in Step 4 (22 x C).

STEP 7
Continue beading around the triangle with 1 bead in all the side spaces and 2 beads in a **Herringbone Increase** on top of everywhere you added 2 beads previously until it's as big as needed.

Step 1

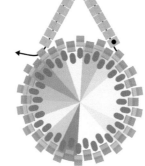

Step 2

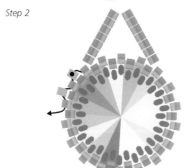

Step 3

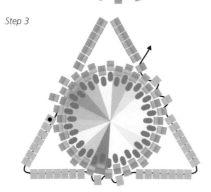

Step 4

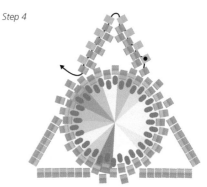

Step 5

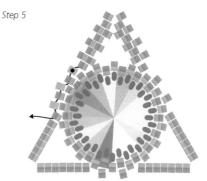

Step 6

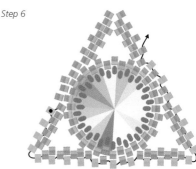

> **TOP TIP**
> *After Step 6 you may find it easier to weave to exit the first bead of the Herringbone Increase pair in the next corner so you always begin in the corner*

> **TOP TIP**
> *You can add a **Star Design** to your Rivoli if you wish*

> **12MM RIVOLI VARIATION**
> *This is beaded using the same technique as the 14mm Rivoli but with some changes to the numbers of beads picked up/ added:*
> - *In Steps 1 and 3 you'll only pick up 10 C beads in your loops and then count along just 3 beads in the central round of C beads*
> - *In steps 4 and 6 you'll only bead 2 single Peyote Stitches into each side of the loops*

Full Rivoli Triangles

Full Rivoli Triangles have no space between the Rivoli and the extra beading. This makes for a different look but an extra layer of complication to the beadwork...

STEP 1
Bezel a 14mm Rivoli using the **Basic Bezelling Instructions**. Exit a C bead on the central round of C beads.

STEP 2
Pick up 2 x C beads. Thread into the next bead in the same round as you are exiting (2C)

STEP 3
Change direction. Pick up 1 x C and thread back through the last bead just added. Pick up 2 x C beads and add them using a **Herringbone Increase** (Page 96) by threading into the first bead picked up in Step 2.
Pick up 1 x C and thread into the bead you were exiting in the base round in Step 1. Thread through it in the same direction as you previously did (4 x C).

STEP 4
Weave through your base to exit the next C bead along in the same round on your base - with your needle facing in the same direction as it was to start.

STEP 5
Peyote Stitch 1 x C twice and then add 2 C (using a **Herringbone Increase**) on top of the 2 added in Step 3. Peyote Stitch using a single bead twice. Finish by entering your base into the next bead along in the same round (6C).

STEP 6
Change direction. Peyote Stitch 1 C into the last bead added. Peyote Stitch a single C into the next 2 spaces. Add 2 x C (using a **Herringbone Increase**) on top of the 2 added in Step 5. Peyote stitch using a single C three times. Finish by threading into the bead you were exiting in the base round in Step 4. Thread through it in the same direction as you previously did.

STEP 7
Weave along the central round of C beads, leaving 5 spaces (from where you added the pair of C beads in Step 1) and then repeat Steps 1-6 to add another Triangle Point.

TOP TIP
*You can also add a **Star Design** to your Rivoli*

STEP 8
Repeat Step 7 to add the 3rd Triangle Point.

STEP 9
You can now bead around the edges of the triangle you have created, increasing just as you would a regular triangle.

TOP TIP
*After Step 8 you may find it easier to weave to exit a **Herringbone Increase** in any of what are now your corners so that you always begin each round in the corner*

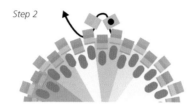
Step 2

Step 3

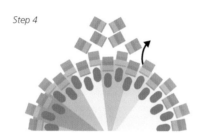
Step 4

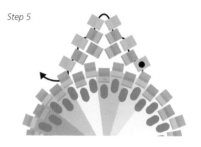
Step 5

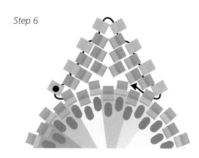
Step 6

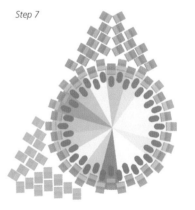
Step 7

Step 8

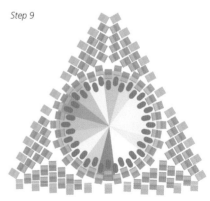
Step 9

Open Rivoli Triangles Necklace

Unite geometric & sparkling components for endless possibilities...

Materials
- 6 x 14mm Rivolis
- 3g of size 15 Miyuki seed beads - S15 beads
- 8g of size 11 Cylinder beads - C beads
- Optional - fine jump rings
- Chain or stringing materials of choice

I used
- Rivolis: Crystal Paradise Shine, Emerald and Crystal Green Sphinx
- Seed beads: Miyuki #457
- Cylinders: DB103

Techniques
- Basic Bezelling Technique, Page 12
- Beaded Tabs, Page 20
- Beading A Triangle, Page 96
- Zipping & Joining Triangles, Page 97
- Open Rivoli Triangles, Page 100
- Peyote Stitch

THE STEPS...

STEP 1

Following the instructions for beading **Open Rivoli Triangles** and **Zipping & Joining Triangles,** bead as many triangles as desired and join them together.

STEP 2

To turn it into a necklace, either link jump rings through any top corner Cylinder bead and then attach your chain to this or bead Tabs along the top edge and thread a chain or jump rings through them (see the **Large Rivoli Triangles Necklace** for an example of this).

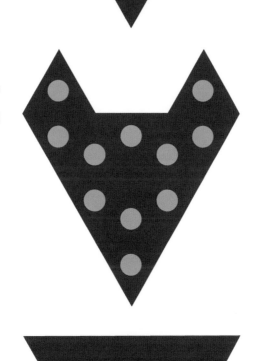

The finished necklace shown is just one way you can zip together Open Rivoli Triangles to make a finished piece. Here are some other examples and look throughout this chapter to find other ways triangles are joined to make shapes and finished pieces. You'll find bracelets, pendants, long strips, pyramids... and more!

VARIATIONS
*You can also bead this necklace with **Open Rivoli Triangles, 'Plain Triangles'** or even the prin*ciple used in **Layered Triangle Pendant**.

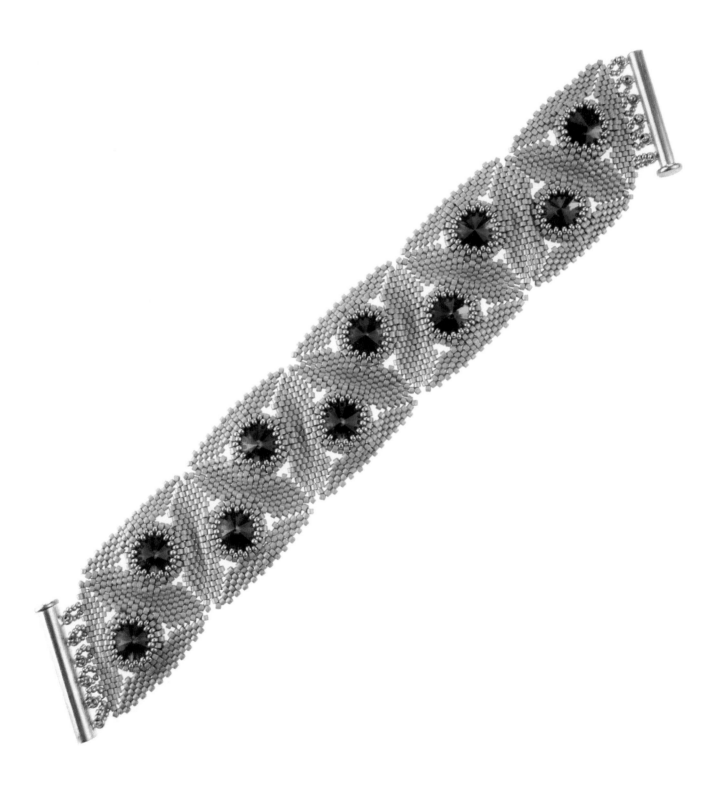

Slanted Bracelet
Unite Triangles for a sparkling bracelet

Materials

For a bracelet to fit 8 inches/ 20cm

- 10 x 12mm Rivolis
- 3g of size 15 Miyuki seed beads - S15 beads
- 10g of size 11 Cylinder beads - C beads
- 6-loop slider clasp

I used

- Rivolis: Emerald
- Seed beads: Miyuki #4204
- Cylinders: DB1153

Techniques

- Basic Bezelling Technique (12mm), Page 15
- Beading a Triangle, Page 96
- Zipping & Joining Triangles, Page 97
- Open Rivoli Triangles (12mm), Page 100
- Peyote Stitch

THE STEPS...

STEP 1

Following the instructions for a **Basic Rivoli Bezel (12mm Rivoli)**, **Beading Open Rivoli Triangles (12mm Rivoli Variation)** and **Beading a Triangle** bezel a Rivoli and add 3 more Increasing Rounds to bring it up to 12 beads a side.

STEP 2

Add a Point Round to this first Triangle and put to one side.

STEP 3

Repeat Step 1 to make another triangle and then zip it to the first.

STEP 4

Repeat Step 3 to make 8 more triangles and join them all together in a line.

STEP 5

Attaching the clasp.

The clasp is attached by using S15 beads coming out of C beads in the Point Rounds of your end triangles. You'll need to do this by eye as each clasp will have its loops at slightly different places.

You may also find that your S15 beads fit through the loops in your clasp which means you can pick up a single strand of beads for each one and then thread through the loop, or you may need to pick up some beads, thread through the loop, and then pick up the rest of the beads.

So, weave to exit an appropriate C bead at the edge of your work and then pick up as many S15s as needed and thread into the appropriate loop on your clasp. Circle back through the C bead and then weave to exit the next appropriate one. Repeat this until all one side of the clasp is attached and then repeat at the other end of your bracelet to finish.

TOP TIP

It is very important before finishing the second end of your bracelet to make sure your clasp is added on so it will work!

The easiest way to do this is to fasten the clasp and bead onto it when it's closed

TOP TIP

These instructions cover how I attached my clasp, but feel free to experiment with other clasps and other methods

SIZING

Sizing is an issue with this bracelet. As it needs an even number of triangles to make it work, you can't simply add or remove single triangles to adjust the length.

- *If you want to make it longer you can add at least 1 extra round per triangle*
- *To make it shorter then add fewer Increasing Rounds*
- *Using a different clasp will mean you can play around with the sizing a bit more*
- *Using more or less seed beads to attach your clasp will adjust the length*

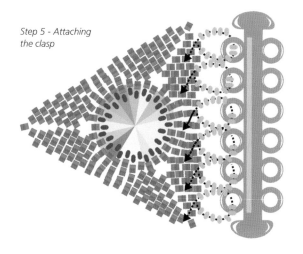

Step 5 - Attaching the clasp

Rivoli Bunting
Fly the flag for Rivolis with these sparkling pendants!

Materials
Each single-sided bunting needs:
- 1 x 14mm Rivoli
- 1g of size 15 Miyuki seed beads - S15s
- 1g of size 11 cylinder beads in main colour - C1 beads
- 1g of size 11 cylinder beads in highlight colour - C2 beads

Each double-sided bunting needs:
- 2 x 14mm Rivolis
- 1g of size 15 Miyuki seed beads - S15s
- 2g of size 11 cylinder beads in main colour - C1 beads
- 2g of size 11 cylinder beads in highlight colour - C2 beads

I used
- Rivolis: Olivine, Denim Blue and Peridot
- Seed beads: Miyuki #4206
- Cylinder beads: DB208 (C1) and DB1832 (C2)

Techniques
- Stitch-In-The-Ditch, Page 11
- Beaded Tabs, Page 20
- Beading a Triangle, Page 96
- Geometric Basics, Page 96
- Full Rivoli Triangles, Page 101
- Peyote Stitch

SINGLE-SIDED BUNTING

STEP 1
Using C1 beads follow Steps 1-9 of **Full Rivoli Triangle** then add 3 more Increasing Rounds (the last one in C2 beads) until your Triangle has 14 beads per side.

STEP 2
Using C2 beads add a Point Round and following the instructions under **Playing With Bezels** or **Large Rivoli Triangle Necklace** bead a tab to hang it from.

DOUBLE-SIDED BUNTING

STEP 1
Using your C1 beads follow Steps 1-9 of **Full Rivoli Triangle** and then add 3 more Increasing Rounds (the last one in C2 beads) until your Triangle has 14 beads per side and then add a Point Round (also in C2 beads).

TOP TIP
Be sure to pull tight (and to the back!) as you bead the 3 'plain rounds' in Step 2 so that your work 'cups up' and develops sides/ depth

STEP 2
Using C2 beads, and Peyote Stitch with 1 x C in every space, add 3 more rounds.

STEP 3
Repeat Step 1 but all in C2 beads and then zip your two pieces together, back to back.

STEP 4
Following the instructions under **Playing With Bezels** or **Large Rivoli Triangle Necklace** bead a tab to hang it from.

Variations

- You can add more or fewer rounds to your Triangles as desired, just make sure each side matches in size
- **Open Rivoli Triangles**, **Full Rivoli Triangles**, **Triangle Bezels** and the principle used in **Layered Triangle Pendant**, can all be used as the Triangles in Bunting. You can even just bead 'plain triangles' for one side if wanted

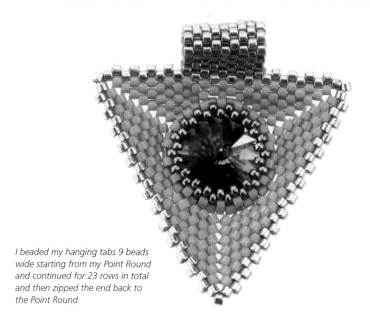

I beaded my hanging tabs 9 beads wide starting from my Point Round and continued for 23 rows in total and then zipped the end back to the Point Round

Rivoli Triangle Heart

Show off your love for Rivolis with this beaded heart!

Materials
Each Heart uses:
- 1 x 14mm Rivoli
- 1g of size 15 Miyuki seed beads - S15s
- 2g of size 11 cylinder beads - C beads

I used
- Rivoli: Crystal Brandy
- Seed beads: Miyuki #4203
- Cylinder beads: DB735

Techniques
- Geometric Basics, Page 96
- Full Rivoli Triangles, Page 101
- Peyote Stitch

THE STEPS...

STEP 1
Using your C beads follow Steps 1-9 of **Full Rivoli Triangle** and then add 1 more Increasing Round so your Triangle has 12 beads per side.

STEP 2
Bead an Increasing Round but don't put a bead in the centre space on one side. Instead, on that side, you'll add 5 x 1C, then leave the next space empty by weaving through previous rounds to ensure no thread is left in the space, and then add 5 x 1C again (38 x C).

STEP 3
Bead an Increasing round but add nothing in the space you left a bead out of last time, and again weave up and down previous rounds to do this (40 x C).

STEP 4
First Heart Lobe.
Add nothing in the corner and then Peyote Stitch 5 single C beads before turning to exit the last new bead added (5 x C).

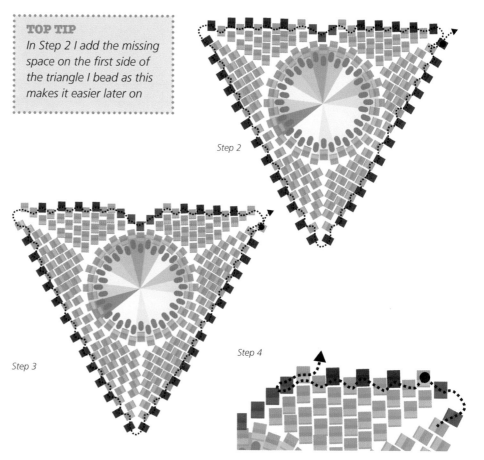

> **TOP TIP**
> In Step 2 I add the missing space on the first side of the triangle I bead as this makes it easier later on

Step 2

Step 3

Step 4

> **TOP TIP**
> The diagrams use 2 different colours to show you where you can add an outline to your heart if desired.
> If you do want an outline then you need to begin it right back at Step 1 (when beading the triangle it is worked on). When you're beading the **Full Rivoli Triangle**, at Step 9, add a single Outline bead at the centre of one edge. Then when beading the next Increasing Round add an outline bead either side of it

> **TOP TIP**
> After Step 3 you'll begin to bead each Heart Lobe separately rather than weave around the entire piece. To do the necessary turning & repositioning you can weave through the beads in your work, but I prefer instead to loop my working thread (black in the diagram) around a previous thread that is right where I am (red in the diagram) and reverse to exit the last bead added. Pull gently to check it has held and then you can continue beading

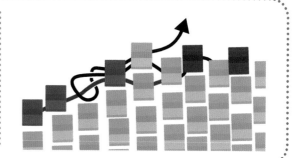

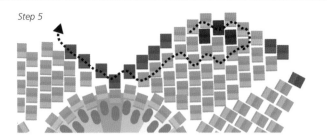

Step 5

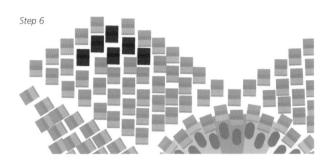

Step 6

> **TOP TIP**
> *If beading an Outlined Heart then, during Step 5, you might want to add in a row with a single C in your Outline colour to ensure a full outline around the edge*

STEP 5

Finishing the first Heart Lobe.
Add a row with 4 single C beads, then a row with 3 single C beads, and lastly a row with 2 single C beads before weaving through your work ready to bead the next Heart Lobe (9 x C).

STEP 6

Bead the other Heart Lobe with rows of 5, 4, 3 and lastly 2 beads (14 x C).

STEP 7

Extending The Heart Point.
Weave to exit the corner after the second Heart Lobe and add nothing in this corner but move onto the next space. Add 13 single C beads, a **Herringbone Increase** in the bottom corner and then 13 single C beads. Turn as before to exit the last bead added (28 x C).

STEP 8

Add 27 single C beads including just 1 on the bottom corner (27 x C).

STEP 9

Add a Hanging Loop at the back and wear your love of Rivolis with pride!

> **Variations**
>
> Any style of Triangle in this book can be used as the basis of a Rivoli Heart. You just need to bead it to 12 beads a side and then start at Step 2

Step 7

Step 8

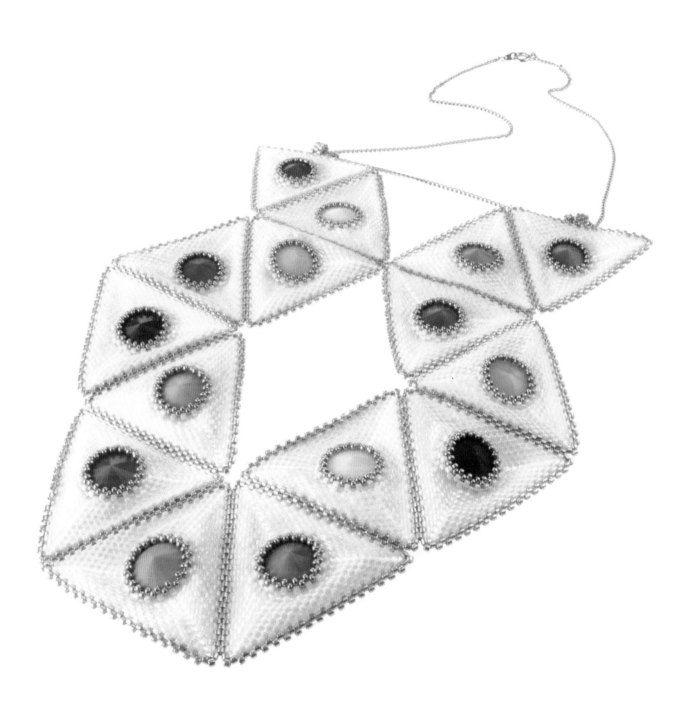

Large Rivoli Triangle Necklace
Get BIG & BOLD with this striking beaded necklace

Materials
- 15 x 14mm Rivolis
- 9g of size 15 Miyuki seed beads - S15 beads
- 40g of size 11 Cylinder beads in main colour- C1 beads
- 7g of size 11 Cylinder beads in triangle edging colour- C2 beads
- 1 chain

I used
- Seed beads: Miyuki #4204
- C1 beads: DB203
- C2 beads: DB1832
- Rivolis (all Matubo): Pink Opal, Green Turquoise, Wasabi, Dark Alabaster green, Opaque Yellow, Opaque Blue, Aqua Satin, Opaque Sky Blue, Light Mint, Violet, Coral, Light Opaque Yellow, Chocolate Blue, Goldenrod and Brown Pearl

Techniques
- Basic Bezelling Technique, Page 12
- Adding Star Designs, Page 16
- Beaded Tabs, Page 20
- Beading a Triangle, Page 96
- Zipping & Joining Triangles, Page 97
- Full Rivoli Triangles, Page 101
- Peyote Stitch

THE STEPS...

STEP 1
Following the instructions for **Basic Bezelling Technique, Adding Star Designs** (optional) and **Full Rivoli Triangles** use C1 beads to turn one of your Rivolis into a Full Triangle.

STEP 2
Continue beading and increasing your Triangle, using C1 beads, until there are 16 beads per side.

STEP 3
Bead one increasing round using C2 beads to make 17 beads per side.

STEP 4
Add a Point Round in C2 beads by adding 1 bead into every space.

STEP 5
Repeat Steps 1-4 to bezel a 2nd Rivoli and zip it to any side of the 1st making sure to fill in the rest of the Point Round on the new Rivoli Full Triangle.

TOP TIP
I used Rivolis which are the same colour on both sides (mostly) so that I could make the whole piece reversible by adding the **Star Design** to one side of each.
To do this I bezelled each Rivoli using the basic instructions but only added 2 rounds of S15 beads at the 'back' as they were held in securely by then

SIZING
This is a big necklace with the beadwork measuring 7 inches/ 17cm tall by 5 ½ inches/ 14cm wide. If you want to scale it down you can do less increasing on each triangle or add less triangles

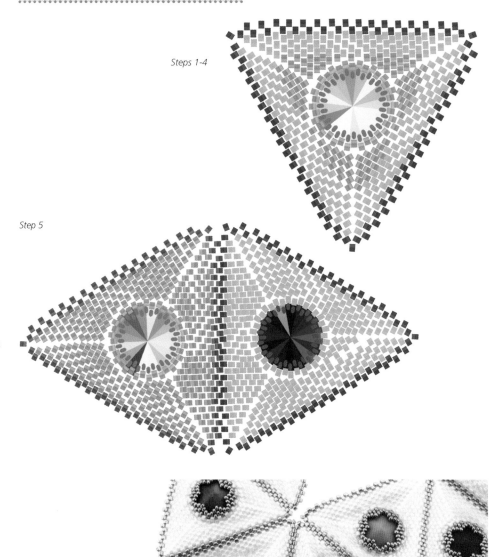

Steps 1-4

Step 5

By using Rivolis with no coating on the back (mostly) I could make a reversible piece by adding the Star Design to one side of each Rivoli

To wear the necklace, simply thread a chain through the tabs. If you find that the beadwork slides or bunches up on the chain, you can tie knots in it which sit on the inner edges of each tab so when worn they slide to the tabs and stop the beadwork from moving around on the chain.

STEP 6

Repeat Steps 1-4 to bezel a 2nd Rivoli and zip it to any side of the 1st making sure to fill in the rest of the Point Round on the new **Full Rivoli Triangle**.

STEP 7

Continue bezelling Rivolis and adding them to the previous ones in the pattern shown until you have 13 of them joined (not the top 2 on both sides in the finished necklace – just what is shown in the diagram). If you want, you can join the point beads of the 2 triangles which touch each other towards the middle centre of the necklace so they sit straight when worn.

STEP 8

You will now bezel the last 2 Rivolis and zip them to the rest of the necklace. As you do this you'll bead the tabs which your chain will thread through.
After adding the Point Round on one of the last 2 Rivolis, count in 8 x C2 beads from one end on the top edge. Add 1 x C2 using Peyote Stitch and then change direction and add a row of 2 x C2 beads using Odd-Count Peyote Stitch. Continue until you've added a total of 15 rows and then fold the tab over and zip it to the Point Round. Do the same on the last Full Triangle as you zip it into place.

Step 7

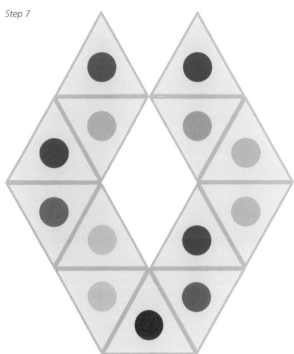

Step 8

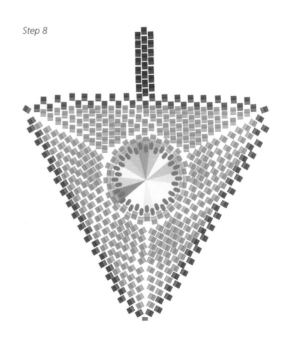

Variations

Any style (and size) of Triangle in this book can be used as the basis of a version of this necklace

TOP TIP

The necklace can have a beaded rope or strands of beads attached to it so you can wear it or you can use beaded tabs to thread a purchased chain through as in the instructions

Rivoli Teardrops Set

These variations on Rivoli Full Triangles are perfect for joining together for different shapes & pieces of jewellery

Materials

For each Rivoli Teardrop:
- 1 x 14mm Rivoli
- 1g of size 15 Miyuki seed beads - S15s
- 1g of size 11 Cylinder beads - C beads
- Findings as appropriate

I used
- Rivolis: Emerald Pastel
- Seed beads: Miyuki #4203
- C beads: DB1832

Techniques
- Basic Rivoli Bezel, Page 12
- Beading Tabs, Page 20
- Beading a Triangle, Page 96
- Full Rivoli Triangles, Page 101
- Peyote Stitch

THE STEPS...

STEP 1

The base shape.
Follow the instructions for a **Basic Rivoli Bezel, Adding a Star Design** (optional) and Steps 1-6 of **Full Rivoli Triangles** stopping when you have added just 1 triangle point to your Rivoli.

STEP 2

The Point Round.
Add a single C bead into each space (22C).

Step 1

Step 2

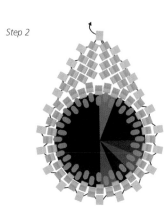

TOP TIP - THE POINT ROUND

Not all of the beads in the Point Round are necessary to zip Teardrops together. All those which are purely decorative are purple in this diagram. The only ones you need for zipping are the 7 green ones in the diagram (1 in the tip and 3 on each side of the tip)

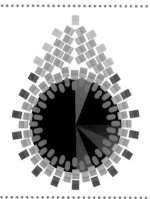

EARRINGS

The simplest way to turn your Teardrops into finished pieces is to either use the 'Tip' bead in the Point Round of your Teardrop to attach a jump ring or finding to, or, as I did with the earrings shown, pick up an earring finding in that spot instead of a bead

Pendant

Simply bead a tab (using Ladder Stitch) coming from the Tip bead to thread a chain through

Ring

You can bead a much longer tab (or strip of Ladder-Stitched beads) starting and ending in a round of C beads at the back of your bezel, to enable a Teardrop to be used as a finger or scarf ring. Start at one side and bead it as long as needed before zipping to the other edge or start 2, one at either side of your Rivoli, and then zip them together in the middle (this method will make it easier for you to size it if it's to be a finger ring)

BACK

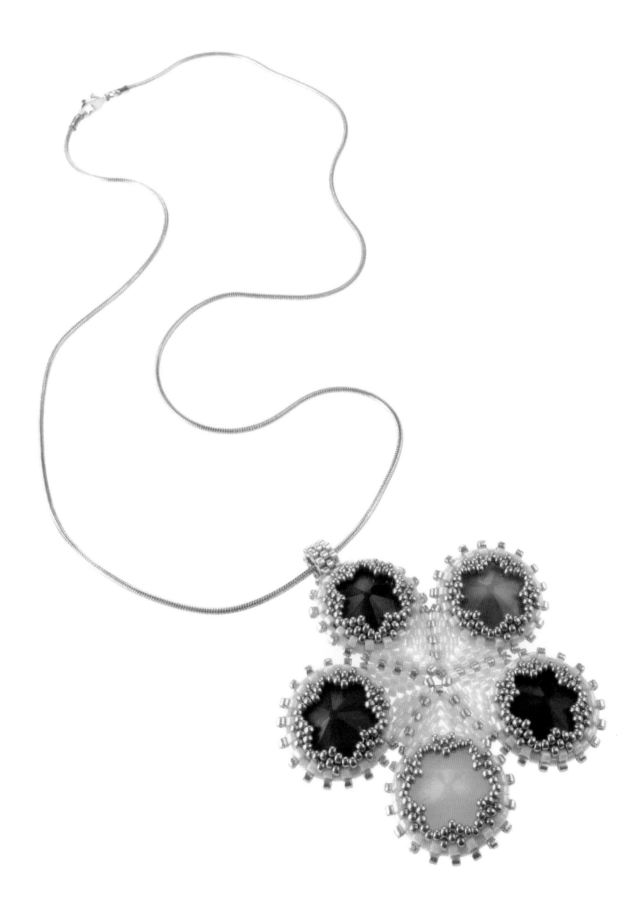

Full Circle Teardrop Pendant

Materials
- 5 x 14mm Rivolis
- 2g of size 15 Miyuki seed beads - S15s
- 3g of size 11 Cylinder beads in main colour - C1 beads
- 2g of size 11 Cylinder beads in teardrop edging colour - C2 beads

I used
- Seed beads: Miyuki #4204
- C1 beads: DB203
- C2 beads: DB1832
- Rivolis (all Matubo): Sky Blue Pearl, Capri Blue, Leaf Green, Dark Violet and Mulberry Pearl

Techniques
- Basic Bezelling Technique, Page 12
- Adding Star Designs, Page 16
- Beaded Tabs, Page 20
- Beading a Triangle, Page 96
- Zipping & Joining Triangles, Page 97
- Full Rivoli Triangles, Page 101
- Rivoli Teardrops Set, Page 114
- Peyote Stitch

THE STEPS...

STEP 1
The first Teardrop.
Bead Steps 1-2 of **Rivoli Teardrops Set** using C1 beads for Step 1 and C2 beads for Step 2. It is up to you whether you add in all of the Point Round beads or just the 7 needed for zipping (I added all of them in mine).

STEP 2
Bead a second Rivoli Teardrop and zip it onto the first using the 3 Point Round beads on one side of the first Teardrop, near the pointed end. Make sure you fill in the rest of the Point Round on the 2nd teardrop (even if just the one in the Tip and those needed for the next to zip to).

STEP 3
Bead 2 more Rivoli teardrops and zip them to the others forming a circle as you go.

STEP 4
Bead one last Rivoli Teardrop and zip it between the 4th and 1st ones making sure to fill in the rest of the Point Round beads, even if it is only the single bead at the Tip.

STEP 5
Adding the Hanging Tab.
This can be added to any of your individual Rivoli Teardrops. Weave to exit the C" bead either side of the central C" bead on the outer edge of any of your Teardrops. Using C2 beads and Peyote Stitch add 2 x 1C (2C).

STEP 6
Weave through your work to exit the last C added and Peyote Stitch 1C. Using Odd-Count Peyote Stitch with 1 or 2 x C2 beads per row add 13 more rows for a total of 15 (if you want to use a thicker hanging material you can add more rows as needed).

STEP 7
Fold the Tab over and zip the last row to the beads in the last row of the original Teardrop.

Variations
- You can embellish the edges of your teardrops with extra beads such as seed or drops for added texture

- I used Rivolis with no coating on the back so I could add a **Star Design** to one side of them. If your Rivolis have a coating then you can choose whether or not to add a **Star Design**, or add it to just some of the Rivolis

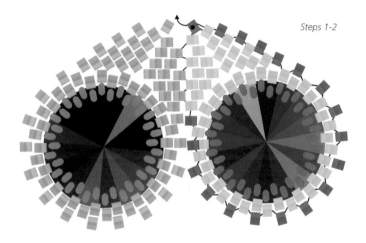

Steps 1-2

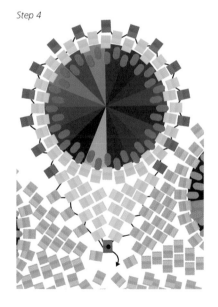

Step 4

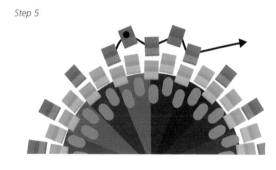

Step 5

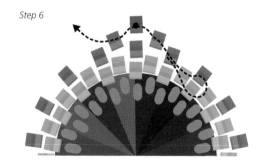

Step 6

Half Circle Teardrop Pendant

Materials
- 3 x 14mm Rivolis
- 2g of size 15 Miyuki seed beads - S15s
- 2g of size 11 Cylinder beads in main colour- C1 beads
- 1g of size 11 Cylinder beads in teardrop edging colour- C2 beads

I used
- Seed beads: Miyuki #4204
- C1 beads: DB203
- C2 beads: DB1832
- Rivolis (all Matubo): Capri Blue, Light Opaque Yellow and Green Turquoise

Techniques
- Basic Bezelling Technique, Page 12
- Adding Star Designs, Page 16
- Beaded Tabs, Page 20
- Beading a Triangle, Page 96
- Zipping & Joining Triangles, Page 97
- Full Rivoli Triangles, Page 101
- Rivoli Teardrop Set, Page 114
- Peyote Stitch

THE STEPS...

STEP 1
The first Teardrop.
Bead Steps 1-2 of the **Rivoli Teardrop Set** using C1 beads for Step 1 and C2 beads for Step 2. It is up to you whether you add in all of the Point Round beads or just the 7 needed for zipping (in mine I only added in the bead in the 'corner' at the tip and 3 either side of that). Leave the thread to use to add your Tab later.

STEP 2
Bead a second Rivoli Teardrop and zip it onto the first using the 3 Point Round beads on one side of the original Teardrop nearest the pointed end. If you want to you can 'ladder on' an extra C2 bead between the 2 teardrops right after the Zipping ends. Make sure you fill in the rest of the Point Round on the 2nd teardrop.

STEP 3
Bead 1 more Rivoli Teardrop and zip it to the 2nd one.

STEP 4
Adding the Hanging Tabs.
These are added to both of the end Teardrops. On either of the Teardrops weave to exit the C2 added in the Point Round furthest from the Point.

STEP 5
Using Peyote Stitch add 1 x C (1C).

STEP 6
Reverse direction and Peyote Stitch 1C and then thread down 1 more C in the row below.
Reverse direction and Peyote Stitch 1C and again thread down 1 more C in the row below.
Reverse direction and Step-Up into the first new bead added in this Step (2 x C).

STEP 7
Repeat Steps 5-6 until your Tab is as long as desired. Fold the Tab over and zip the last row to the beads in the last row of the original Teardrop. Bead a second tab on the other edge Teardrop.

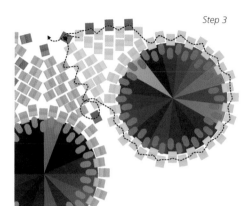
Step 3

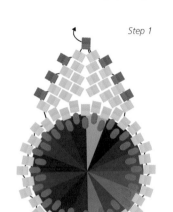
Step 1

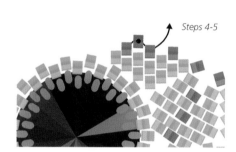
Steps 4-5

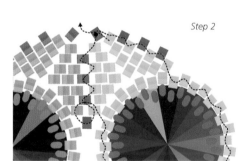
Step 2

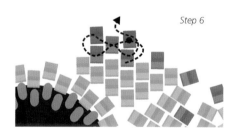
Step 6

Variations

- Joining in another Teardrop gives you a 'pie with a slice taken out' shape which looks much better worn than described!

- You can embellish the edges of the teardrops with beads such as seed or drops for extra texture

- My Rivolis had no coating on the back so I was able to add a **Star Design** to one side of them and make a reversible piece. If your Rivolis have a coating then you can choose whether or not to add a **Star Design** or add it to just some of the Rivolis

Triangle Bezel
Get geometric to adorn your Rivolis

TOP TIP
These can also be used instead of **Open Rivoli Triangles** *or* **Full Rivoli Triangles** *to make necklaces, bracelets, bunting etc...*

Materials
- 1 x 14mm Rivoli
- 1g of size 11 Cylinder beads - C beads

Techniques
- Peyote Stitch Decrease, Page 11
- Geometric Basics, Page 96
- Peyote Stitch

THE STEPS...

STEP 1
Rounds 1-2 - The Base Circle.
Pick up 48 x C and thread through 6 to join into a circle (this leaves your tail in the right spot to continue later (48 x C).

STEP 2
Rounds 3-5.
Using Peyote Stitch, and 1 x C in each space, add 3 rounds until you have a total of 5 (24 x C each round).

STEP 3
Round 6 – First decreasing round.
*Add 1 x C into 7 spaces and then bead a **Peyote Stitch Decrease** in the next space*. Repeat from * to * twice more then Step-Up to exit the first bead added (21 x C).

STEP 4
Round 7 – Second decreasing round.
*Add 1 x C into 6 spaces and then bead a **Peyote Stitch Decrease** in the next space*. Repeat from * to * twice more and then Step-Up to exit the first bead added (18 x C).

TOP TIP
As you bead decreases make sure they line up with previous ones

STEP 5
Round 8 – Third decreasing round.
*Add 1 x C into 5 spaces then bead a **Peyote Stitch Decrease** in the next space*. Repeat from * to * twice more then Step-Up to exit the first bead added (15 x C).

STEP 6
Reinforcing Round.
Weave all around your work as though beading Step 5 again but threading across the corners between beads added in Step 5 which will hold your Rivoli in tight.

STEP 7
Rounds 9-11.
Either return to your tail thread or weave your working thread to exit the same place it is and then at this edge of your work repeat Steps 3-4. Insert your Rivoli so it faces out of the beads from Steps 3-5 and then repeat Step 5.

STEP 8
Continuing decreasing.
Bead the principle of decreasing rounds until you end up with just 1 bead per side. Weave through these 3 beads to tie together and finish.

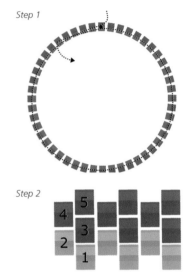
Step 1

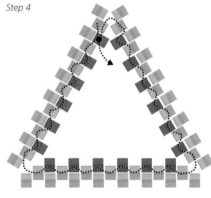
Step 2

Step 3

Step 4

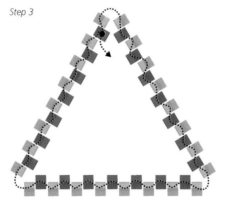
Step 5

Step 6

Step 8

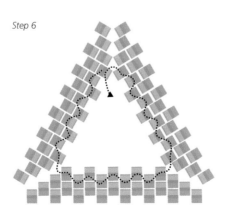

Distorted Square

STEP 1
Round 1.
Pick up 4 x C and tie the thread into a knot and circle through the first bead to join into a ring (4 x C).

> **TOP TIP**
> *As you continue beading pull your work tight as this helps the shape to form and your Square to distort and fold over. Adding a knot when you first pick up the beads helps this to happen*

STEP 2
Round 2 – First increasing round.
Using a **Herringbone Increase**, add a pair of C beads between each bead from the previous step. At the end of the round make sure to Step-Up to exit the first bead added, this will be the first of a pair (8 x C).

> **TOP TIP**
> *The diagrams will show your work as flat when in reality it will begin to fold over so it looks like two 'half-squares' lying on each other rather than a flat square*

STEP 3
Round 3 – Second Increasing Round.
*Using a **Herringbone Increase** (Page 96) add 2 x C between the next 2 x C beads picked up in Step 2 and then, using Peyote Stitch, add 1 x C bead into the next space*. Repeat from * to * three more times and then, at the end of the round, Step-Up to exit the first bead added (it will be the first C bead in the first pair added) (12 x C).

STEP 4
Round 4 onwards.
*Repeat the principle of Step 3 (but with 1 extra single C per side for each round) until as large as desired.

STEP 5
Point Round.
When needed, add a round with just 1 x C in each space, including all the corner spaces.

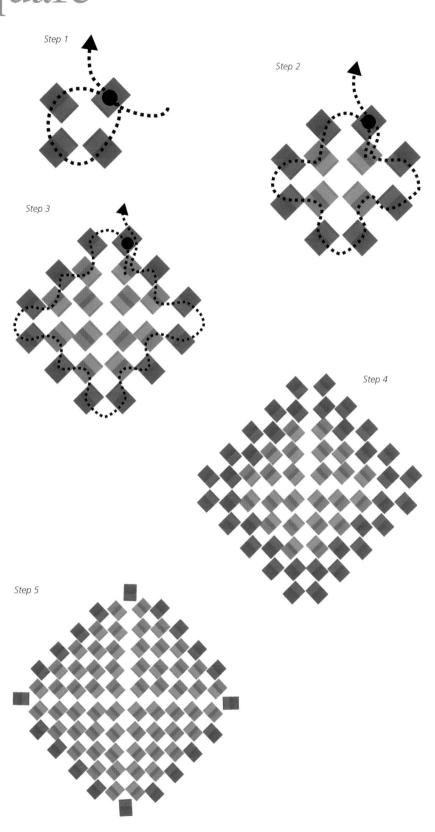

Step 1

Step 2

Step 3

Step 4

Step 5

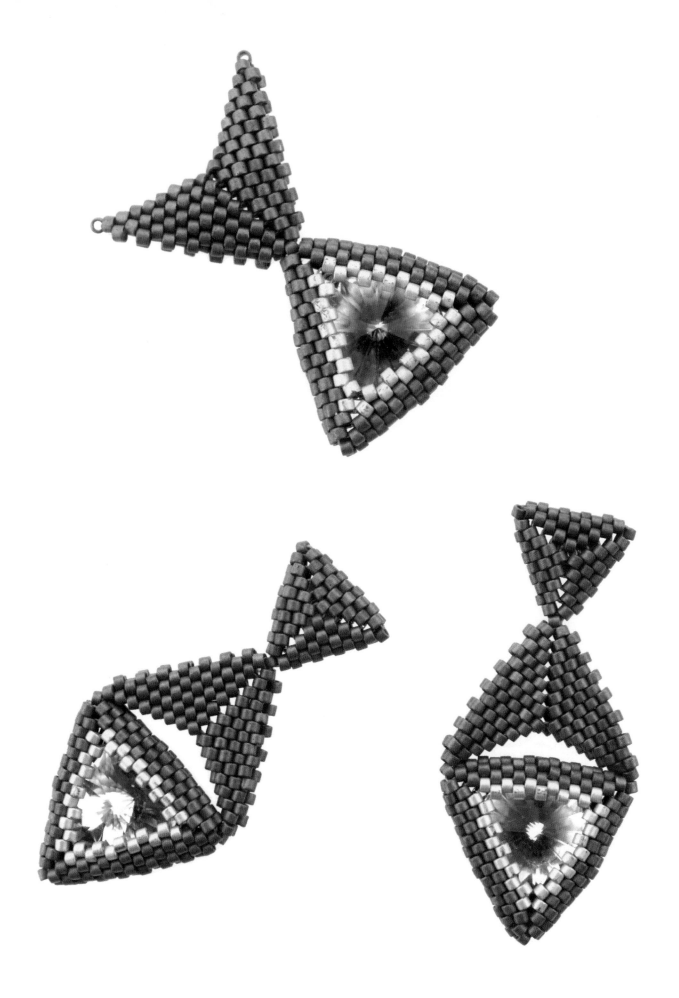

Mixed Shape Set

Materials
- 3 x 14mm Rivolis
- 3g of size 11 cylinder beads - C beads
- Earring posts or other findings of choice

I used
- Rivolis: Violet
- C beads: DB1273 and DB1151

Techniques
- Geometric Basics, Page 96
- Triangle Bezel, Page 120
- Distorted Square, Page 121
- Peyote Stitch

> **TOP TIP**
> *I changed colours for Steps 4-5 on my* **Triangle Bezels** *to create a decorative outline*

> **TOP TIP**
> *These instructions describe how I attached my earring findings, but you can ignore that and simply attach one to a C bead in the top triangle instead*

THE PENDANT
STEP 1
The Bezelled Rivoli.
Follow Step 1-8 of **Triangle Bezel** to bezel a Rivoli and weave away your threads

STEP 2
The Square Bail.
Following the instructions under **Distorted Square,** bead a square until 8 beads a side.

STEP 3
The Point Round.
When adding your Point Round, zip the first corner space in your square to a C bead in a corner of your bezelled triangle (there are 2 beads you can use per corner, use the one nearest the front here). Then fill in 1 side of the Point Round, the 2nd corner and one more side of the Square.
Zip the 3rd corner of the Square to the bead on your triangle which sits behind the one already zipped to.
Fill in the other 2 sides and the 4th corner of the Point Round on your Square and weave away the threads.

EARRINGS
STEP 1
The Bezelled Rivoli.
Follow Step 1-8 of **Triangle Bezel** to bezel a Rivoli and weave away your threads.

STEP 2
The Triangle Top.
Following Steps 1-4 of **Beading a Triangle** (Page 96), begin a triangle and then add 1 more increasing round so you have 5 beads per side.

STEP 3
Following Step 5 of **Beading a Triangle** add a Point Round and then 1 more round with a single bead in each space.

STEP 4
Following the principle of Step 3 of **Triangle Bezel**, bead a decreasing round with just 4 C beads along each side.

STEP 5
Insert your earring finding so it points out of the space where you're beading and then, holding the finding in place, continue decreasing until you have 1 bead per side and weave all around the 3 beads to join them together and finish.

STEP 6
The Distorted Square.
Following the instructions under **Distorted Square,** bead a square until 8 beads a side.

STEP 7
The Point Round.
- You'll zip the first corner space of your square to 2 x C beads in a corner of your bezelled triangle. If you look at the beads in the corner of your Triangle Bezel you'll see there are 2 beads you can use per corner. First thread into the one nearest the front and then thread back up through the one nearest the back and back into your Square.
- Fill in the 1st side of the Point Round on the Square.
- Zip the 2nd corner on the Square to a C bead in a corner of your triangle with the earring finding.

- Fill in the Point Round beads on the 2nd side of your Square.
- Zip the 3rd corner of the Square to your Bezelled Triangle just as you did the 1st corner.
- Fill in the Point Round beads on the 3rd side of your Square.
- Zip the 4th corner of the Square as you did the 2nd (into the triangle with the earring finding) but this time into the corner bead on the Triangle nearer the back.
- Fill in the 4th and last side of your Square and then weave away all threads.

STEP 8
Repeat Steps 1-7 to bead another piece to make a matching pair of earrings.

Step 7

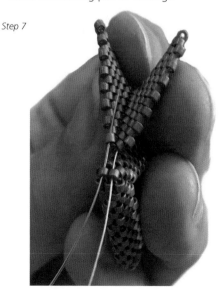

Triple Square Pendant

Materials
- 1 x 14mm Rivoli
- 2g of size 11 cylinder beads - C beads

I used
- Rivolis: Light Colorado Topaz
- C beads: DB1063 and DB1763

Techniques
- Geometric Basics, Page 96
- Triangle Bezel, Page 120
- Distorted Square, Page 121
- Peyote Stitch

THE STEPS...

STEP 1
The Bezelled Rivoli.
Follow Step 1-8 of **Triangle Bezel** to bezel a Rivoli and weave away your threads.

STEP 2
The first Square.
Follow the principle of Steps 6-7 of **Mixed Shape Earrings** to bead a **Distorted Square** and attach it to 2 corners of your Triangle, but on the corners not attached to your Square add a single C bead which you'll add in the 2nd corner and then zip into when beading the 4th.

STEP 3
Repeat Step 2 to bead another Distorted Square and attach it to your Triangle.

STEP 4
Bead another matching Square and attach it to your Triangle but leave the 2nd and 4th corners empty. Then, once the round is beaded, return to those corners to add hanging loops (I added 2 loops, each one beginning from a C bead sitting in the corner at the front and ending in the matching C bead at the back).

> **TOP TIP**
> I changed colours for Steps 4-5 on my bezelled Rivoli and for the last 2 increasing rounds on my Squares (and the Point Round) to create a decorative outline on my work

> **TOP TIP**
> You can also bead a 4th Distorted Square and attach it to any of the others as your bail

Layered Triangle Pendant

Materials
- 1 x 14mm Rivoli
- 2g of size 11 cylinder beads - C beads

I used
- Rivolis: Crystal Metallic Sunshine
- C beads: DB1459 and DB1016

Techniques
- Stitch-In-The-Ditch, Page 11
- Geometric Basics, Page 96
- Triangle Bezel, Page 120
- Peyote Stitch

THE STEPS...

STEP 1
The Bezelled Rivoli.
Follow Step 1-8 of **Triangle Bezel** to bezel a Rivoli.

STEP 2
The Background Triangle.
Weave to exit any bead added in Step 1 of your bezel so that you're in a corner space facing towards the corner. There are 6 possible beads you can use and they all have a red dot on them in the diagram, as well as arrows showing the way you need to exit the bead.

> **TOP TIP**
> *This pendant can also be used as the basis for a Rivoli Heart…*

> **TOP TIP**
> *I changed colours for Steps 4-5 on my bezelled Rivoli to add a decorative outline around my Rivoli*

STEP 3
Using **Stitch-In-The-Ditch**, and the principles of **Beading a Triangle**, add an Increasing Round.

STEP 4
Add 9 more Increasing Rounds until the background Triangle has 18 beads a side (changing colour as desired). Then add a Point Round and following the instructions under **Playing With Bezels** or **Large Rivoli Triangle Necklace**, bead a tab on an outer edge or add a hanging loop to the back.

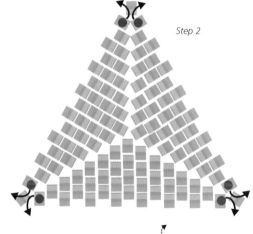

Step 2

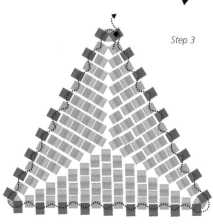

Step 3

Triangle Bezel Pyramids

Take your geometric & Rivoli beading 3-dimensional with these striking pendants

Materials
- 4 or 6 x 14mm Rivolis
- 4g size 11 Cylinder beads - C beads

I used
- Rivolis: Padparadscha, Light Peach, Light Rose, Light Silk and Light Colorado Topaz
- C beads: DB1458, DB1152 and DB1832

Techniques
- Geometric Basics, Page 96
- Triangle Bezel, Page 120
- Layered Triangle Pendant, Page 125
- Peyote Stitch

4-Rivoli Pyramid
STEP 1
The first Triangle - Follow Steps 1-3 of **Layered Triangle Pendant,** to begin and then bead 2 more Increasing Rounds and then a Point Round.

STEP 2
Second Triangle - Repeat Step 1 but,when you reach the Point Round, zip it along one edge to the first Triangle.

STEP 3
Third Triangle - Repeat the previous step but zip this new triangle to sit between the first and second. It only needs one other Point Round side filled in along with all its corner beads.

STEP 4
Fourth Triangle- Repeat Step 1 but this last Triangle needs to be zipped to the other 3 and so only needs new beads added in its 3 corners. Add a Hanging Loop as desired.

6-Rivoli Pyramid
STEP 1
The first Triangle - Follow Steps 1-3 of **Layered Triangle Pendant** to begin BUT as you add the extra beads (in Step 3) do this as a Point Round with 1 bead in each space.

STEP 2
Second Triangle - Repeat Step 1 but, when you reach the Point Round, zip it along one edge to the first Triangle.

STEP 3
Third Triangle - Repeat Step 2 but zip this new triangle to sit between the first and second, so it only needs one other Point Round side filled in and its corner beads.

STEP 4
Fourth Triangle - Repeat Step 1 and zip this Triangle to one side of the first one.

> **VARIATIONS**
> *Any size or style of Triangle in this book can be turned into a pyramid...*

> **TOP TIP**
> *Joining Triangles with just a Point Round beaded on your bezel (as I did in the 6 Rivoli Pyramid) is much harder, so you can add extra increasing rounds if wanted before you do this*

STEP 5
Fifth Triangle- Repeat Step 1 and zip this Triangle to one side of the second one and one side of the fourth one.

STEP 6
Sixth Triangle - Repeat Step 1 and zip this Triangle to one side of the third one and one side each of the fourth and fifth ones (so it only needs its 3 corner C beads). Add a Hanging Loop as desired.

Step 1 of 6-Rivoli Triangle Pyramid

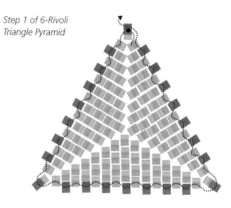

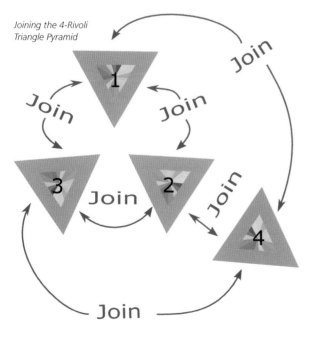

Joining the 4-Rivoli Triangle Pyramid

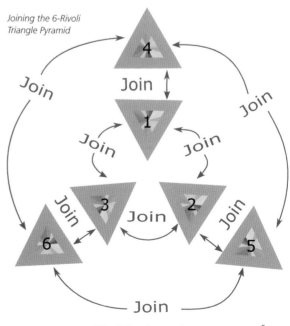

Joining the 6-Rivoli Triangle Pyramid

Flying Vs
A geometric bail creates striking, suspended Rivolis...

These bezelled Rivolis are perfect for creating a mix-and-match piece as they easily slide on and off whatever they're strung on. They're created by combining a Basic Rivoli Bezel with a geometric beaded Distorted Square with a difference – an empty centre. This empty centre (which is optional) allows the stringing material to show through each bail and gives the pieces their unique shape which inspired their name

Materials
For each Flying V:
- 1 x 14mm Rivoli
- 1g of size 15 Miyuki seed beads - S15s
- 1g of size 11 Cylinder beads - C beads

I used
- Rivolis: Dark Moss Green, Olivine, Denim Blue, Peridot, Light Turquoise
- Seed beads: Miyuki #457
- C beads: DB1010
- Stringing material - SilverSllk Pearlesque Gold AB

Techniques
- Basic Bezelling Technique, Page 12
- Herringbone Increase, Page 96
- Distorted Square, Page 121
- Peyote Stitch

THE STEPS...
STEP 1
The base shape.
Following the instructions for the **Basic Bezelling Technique,** bezel a Rivoli and finish all the threads.

STEP 2
Beginning your Square – Rounds 1-2.
On a separate piece of thread pick up 36 x C beads and tie a knot to hold the beads tight and weave to exit any bead (36 x C).

STEP 3
Round 3 – First Increasing Round.
*Using a **Herringbone Increase** add 2 x C between the next 2 x C beads picked up in Step 2 and then, using Peyote Stitch, add 1 x C bead into each of the next 4 spaces*. Repeat from * to * three more times and then, at the end of the round, Step-Up to exit the first bead added (it will be the first C bead in the first pair added) (24 x C).

Step 1

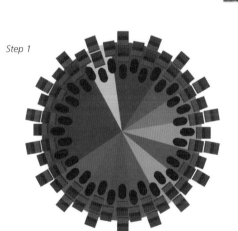

Step 2

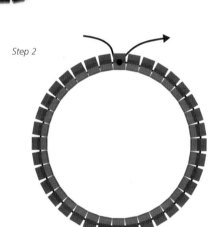

Step 3

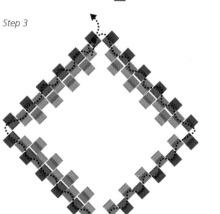

> **TOP TIP**
> As you bead your Square you want to pull your work tight as this helps the shape to form and your Square to distort and fold over. Adding the knot when you first pick up the beads also helps this to happen

> **TOP TIP**
> You can add a **Star Design** to your Rivoli if you wish

STEP 4

Round 4 – Second Increasing Round.
*Using a **Herringbone Increase,** add 2 x
C on top of the 2 x C beads added using a
Herringbone Increase in the last step and
then, using Peyote Stitch, add 1 x C bead
into each of the next 5 spaces*. Repeat from
* to * three more times and then, at the end
of the round, Step-Up to exit the first bead
added (it will be the first C bead in the first
pair added) (28 x C).

STEP 5

Round 5 – Third Increasing Round.
*Using a **Herringbone Increase,** add 2 x
C on top of the 2 x C beads added using a
Herringbone Increase in the last step and
then, using Peyote Stitch, add 1 x C bead
into each of the next 6 spaces*. Repeat from
* to * three more times and then, at the end
of the round, Step-Up to exit the first bead
added (it will be the first C bead in the first
pair added) (32 x C).

STEP 6

Round 6 – Fourth Increasing Round. *Using
a **Herringbone Increase,** add 2 x C on
top of the 2 x C beads added using a
Herringbone Increase in the last step and
then, using Peyote Stitch, add 1 x C bead
into each of the next 7 spaces*. Repeat from
* to * three more times and then, at the end
of the round, Step-Up to exit the first bead
added (it will be the first C bead in the first
pair added) (36 x C).

STEP 7

Round 7 – The Point Round.
* Bring your bezelled Rivoli close and,
  continuing working in the same direction
  as you have been beading, thread into
  any C bead on the front-most round of C
  beads on your bezel. Pull tight to snuggle
  the Bail and the bezel close together.
* Using Peyote Stitch, add 1 x C bead into
  each of the next 17 spaces (including 1
  on top of the pair of C beads added in
  the last round.
* When you reach the 3rd corner; again
  continuing in the same direction as you
  have been beading, thread into the
  matching C bead on the back-most
  round of C beads on your bezel that sits
  behind the C bead already threaded into.
* Using Peyote Stitch, add 1 x C bead into
  each of the next 17 spaces (including 1
  on top of the pair of C beads added in
  the last round.
* Weave around all again to secure and
  weave away your thread to finish (34 x
  C).

TOP TIP
The diagrams will show your Square as flat when in reality it will begin to fold over so it looks like two 'V's lying on each other rather than a flat square

TOP TIP
If you want a bigger 'V' then simply bead more Increasing Rounds like Steps 3-6 before beading the principle of Step 7

Step 4

Step 5

Step 6

Step 7

Variations

If you don't want to leave a gap in the centre of your Square then you can bead a full **Distorted Square** for your bail. See Page 122 for instructions on this

You can also add as many Increasing Rounds as desired before joining to your Rivoli (with or without a filled in centre

To add some extra decoration, and texture, to your work you can use **Stitch-In-The-Ditch** (Page 11) to add some beads to the top of your Square

The edge of your Square can be decorated by using small drop beads, crystals, daggers, seed beads etc.

Extra Sparkle

Adding other crystals to your
Rivolis ramps up the sparkle...

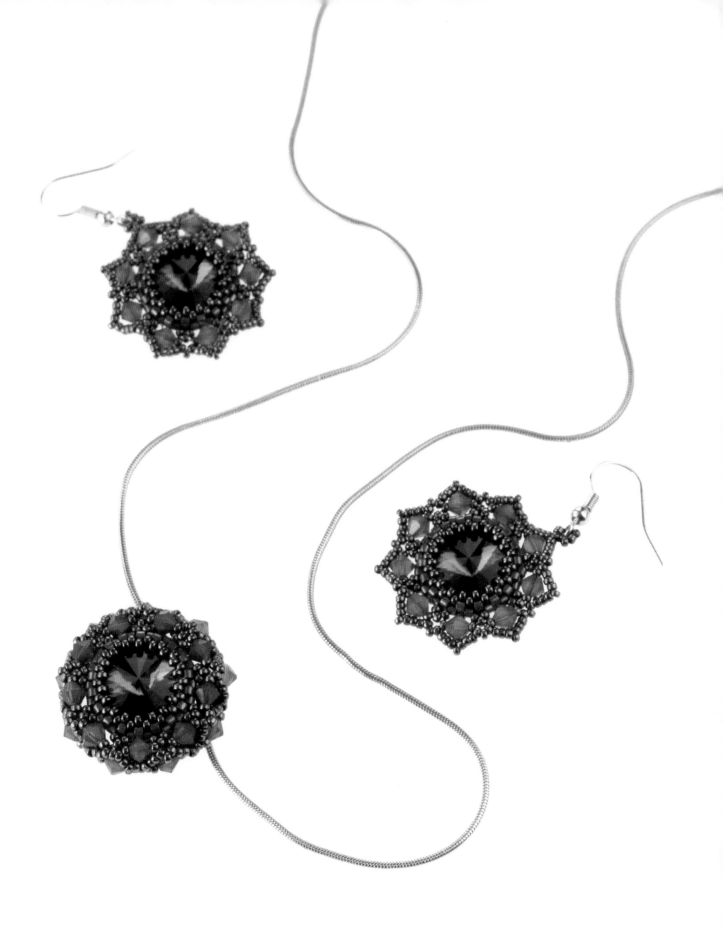

Bicone Snowflakes
The perfect accompaniment for crystals is... more crystals!

These very versatile & variable Bicone Snowflakes are easy to make and ideal for when you want to quickly make pieces using a small amount of bicones. I have described 8 different variations & ways of using them, but do experiment for many more options

Materials
Each Bicone Snowflake uses:
- 1 x 14mm Rivoli
- 1g of size 15 Miyuki seed beads - S15s
- 1g of size 11 cylinder seed beads - C beads
- 9 x 4mm bicones - B beads

Each Deeper Bicone Snowflake uses:
- 1 x 14mm Rivoli
- 1g of size 15 Miyuki seed beads - S15s
- 1g of size 11 cylinder seed beads - Cs
- 18 x 4mm bicones - B beads

I used
- Rivoli: Dark Moss Green
- Seed beads: #457
- Cylinder beads: DB1010
- Bicones: Palace Green Opal

Techniques
- Peyote Stitch Decrease, Page 11
- Stitch-In-The-Ditch, Page 11
- Basic Bezelling Technique, Page 12
- Peyote Stitch
- Netting

THE STEPS...

STEP 1
Bezelling the Rivoli.
Using the **Basic Bezelling Technique** bezel a 14mm Rivoli.

STEP 2
Embellishment - First Round.
Using **Stitch-In-The-Ditch** add 3 x S15 into alternate spaces on the central round of C beads on the bezel. At the end Step-Up to exit the second S15 in any group of 3 (27 x S15).

> **TOP TIP**
> *If you want you can stop after Step 2 for a simple embellished Rivoli*

STEP 3
Embellishment - Second Round.
Pick up 1 x S15, 1B and 1 x S15. Thread into the 2nd S15 in the next group of 3. Repeat 8 more times to add 9 groups of beads and finish by Stepping-Up through 1 x S15, 1 x Bicone and 1 x S15 (18 x S15 and 9 x B).

> **TOP TIP**
> *You can stop after Step 3 for a different look that finishes with a Bicone edging*

STEP 4
Embellishment - Third Round.
Pick up 3 x S15 and, working in the same direction, thread through the next group of S15, B and S15 added in the last step Repeat from * to * 8 more times (27 x S15).

> **TOP TIP**
> *Stopping after Step 4 gives you a piece with extra seed bead embellishment*

Step 1

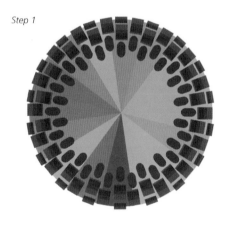

Step 2

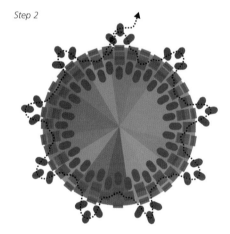

Step 3

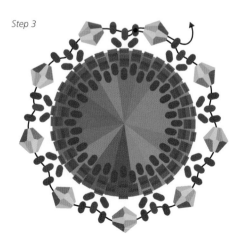

Step 4

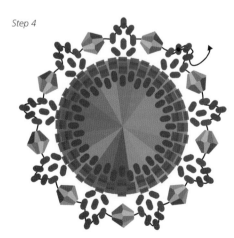

STEP 5

Embellishment - Fourth Round.
Pick up 6 x S15 and, working in the same direction, thread through the next group of 3 x S15 from the last step. Repeat from * to * 8 more times and Step-Up at the end to exit the first 3 x S15s picked up in this step (54 x S15).

> **TOP TIP**
> *Stopping after Step 5 gives you a piece with loops of seed beads framing each bicone*

STEP 6

Embellishment - Fifth Round.
Pick up 1 x S15 and, working in the same direction, thread through the last 3 x S15 from the group of 6 x S15, the 3 x S15s added in Step 4 and then through the first 3 x S15 in the next group of 6. Repeat from * to * 8 more times (9 x S15).

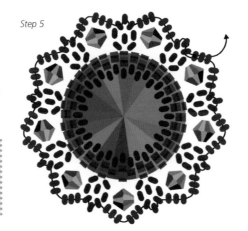

Step 5

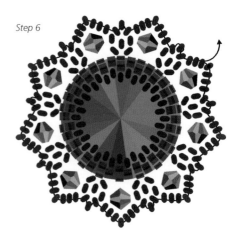

Step 6

Variations

Adding a Hanging Loop at the edge

Weave to exit any S15 added in the last round. Pick up as many S15 beads as needed (thread into an earring finding if appropriate) and circle back through the S15 you were exiting

Adding a Hanging Loop at the back

Whether you've fully covered the back or not, adding a simple loop of S15 beads will allow you to wear your piece as a pendant or brooch

BACK

Deeper Bicone Snowflake

STEP 1
Bead Steps 1-6 of **Bicone Snowflakes** finishing by Stepping-Up to exit one of the S15s added in the last round.

STEP 2
Pick up 2 x S15, 1 x B and 2 x S15s. Thread into the next single S15 added in the last round. Repeat from * to * eight more times then finish by Stepping-Up through one of the groups of beads added (36 x S15 and 9 x Bicones).

STEP 3
Pick up 1 x S15 and thread through the next group of 2 x S15s, 1 x B and 2 x S15s added in the last step. Repeat from * to * eight more times and finish by Stepping-Up to exit any of the single S15s added in this step (9 x S15).

STEP 4 - BROWN IN THE DIAGRAM
You'll now begin to decrease the back. Add groups of 9 x S15s between each S15 added in the last step. Step-Up at the end to exit the 5th bead in any group of 9 (81 x S15).

STEP 5 - BLUE IN THE DIAGRAM
Add groups of 7 x S15 beads threading into the 5th bead in the groups of 9 x S15s from the last step. Step-Up at the end to exit the 4th S15 in any group of 7 (63 x S15).

STEP 6 - YELLOW IN THE DIAGRAM
Add groups of 5 x S15 beads threading into the 4th bead in the groups of 7 x S15s from the last step. Step-Up at the end to exit the 3rd S15 in any group of 5 (45 x S15).

STEP 7 - RED IN THE DIAGRAM
Add groups of 3 x S15 beads threading into the 3rd bead in the groups of 5 x S15s from the last step. Step-Up at the end to exit the 2nd S15 in any group of 3 (27 x S15).

STEP 8 - GREEN IN THE DIAGRAM
Add groups of 3 x S15 beads threading into the 2nd bead in the groups of 3 x S15s from the last step. Step-Up at the end to exit the 2nd S15 in any group of 3 (27 x S15).

STEP 9 - PINK IN THE DIAGRAM
Using Peyote Stitch add single S15 beads threading into the 2nd S15 in each group of 3 from the last step and Step-Up to exit the first bead added (9 x S15).

STEP 10 - BLACK IN THE DIAGRAM
*Using Peyote Stitch add 1 x S15 into the next 2 spaces and then bead a **Peyote Stitch Decrease** in the next space*. Repeat from * to * twice more and finish by Stepping-Up through the first S15 added (6 x S15).

STEP 11 - ORANGE IN THE DIAGRAM
Using Peyote Stitch add 1 x S15 into each space from the last round including 1 over each large space created by the decreases (6 x S15).

STEP 12
Weave all around the 6 x S15s in the last round to secure and finish.

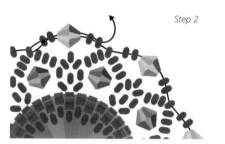

Step 2

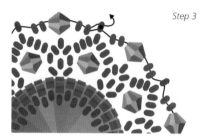

Step 3

Steps 4-12 (this diagram just shows the back of your work and the beads added in Step 2 onwards)

Bicone Bezels

Add extra sparkle with these quick to bead bezels with 3 different variations

Materials

Each Basic Bicone Bezel uses:
- 1 x 14mm Rivoli
- 1g of size 15 Miyuki seed beads - S15s
- 12 x 4mm bicones - B beads

Each Elaborate Bicone Bezel uses:
- 1 x 14mm Rivoli
- 1g of size 15 Miyuki seed beads - S15s
- 18 x 4mm bicones - B beads

Each Simpler Bicone Bezel uses:
- 1 x 14mm Rivoli
- 1g of size 15 Miyuki seed beads - S15s
- 6 x 4mm bicones - B beads

I used
- Rivoli: Yellow Opal
- Seed beads: Miyuki #4203
- Bicones: Amethyst Shimmer x 2

Techniques
- Peyote Stitch Decrease, Page 11
- Hanging Loop, Page 19
- Peyote Stitch

BASIC BICONE BEZEL

STEP 1

The Base Ring.
Pick up 1 x S15 and 1 x B. Repeat this pattern five more times until you have 6 of each and then circle through the first S15 to join into a ring and then weave around the ring again finishing by exiting an S15 (6 x S15 and 6 x C).

STEP 2

Pick up 5 x S15 and thread into the next S15 on the Base Ring. Repeat from * to * five more times and then Step-Up to exit the 3rd S15 added (30 x S15).

STEP 3

Pick up 2 x S15, 1B and 2 x S15 and thread into the 3rd S15 in the next 5-bead loop added in the last step. Repeat from * to * five more times and then Step-Up to exit the first B added (24 x S15 and 6 x B).

STEP 4

Using Peyote Stitch add 1 x S15 into each of the next 3 spots with the last once taking you into the next B added in the last step. Repeat from * to * five more times and then Step-Up to exit the first S15 added (18 x S15).

TOP TIP

When you bead steps 5-7, pull tight and let your work 'cup' up so that it gets depth and begins to make the shape that will hold your Rivoli in. It doesn't matter in which direction you let it cup, but this will determine the front and back of your bezel

STEP 5

Using Peyote Stitch add 1 x S15 into each of the next 2 spaces and then pick up 5 x S15 and thread into the S15 after the Bicone. Repeat from * to * five more times. Step-Up at the end to exit the first S15 added (42 x S15).

Step 1

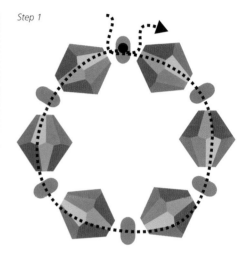

Step 2

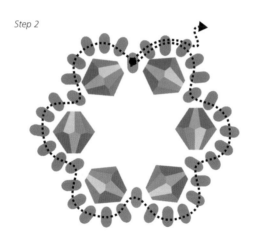

Step 3

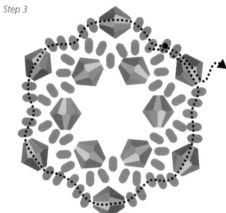

Step 4

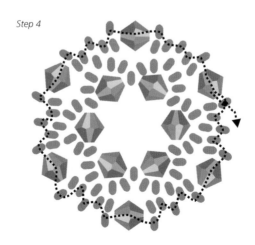

Step 5

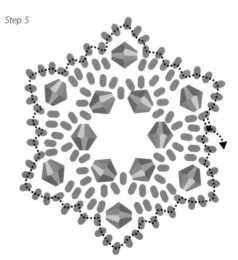

STEP 6

Using Peyote Stitch add 1 x S15 and thread into the next S15 added in the last step, through all the S15s in the 5-bead loop and lastly into the next S15 added in the last step (you'll thread through 7 x S15s in total as you do this). Repeat from * to * five more times and Step-Up to exit the first S15 added (6 x S15).

> **TOP TIP**
> *Your work will now begin to decrease and the diagrams will just show the beads added in Step 5 and onwards*

STEP 7

Pick up 2 x S15 and thread into the 3rd S15 in the next 5-bead loop. Pick up 2 x S15 and thread into the next single S15 added in the last step. Repeat from * to * five more times (pulling tight so the 5-bead loops fold to the back of your work to soon sit behind the Rivoli) and Step-Up to exit the first pair of S15s added (24 x S15).

STEP 8

Insert your Rivoli so it faces out of the beads added in Steps 1-2. Using Peyote Stitch add 1 x S15 between each pair added in the last step (12 x S15).

STEP 9 - ORANGE IN THE DIAGRAM

Using Peyote Stitch add 1 x S15 between each S15 added in the last step (12 x S15).

STEP 10 - BLUE IN THE DIAGRAM

Using Peyote Stitch add 1 x S15 between each S15 added in the last step (12 x S15).

STEP 11 - RED IN THE DIAGRAM

*Using Peyote Stitch add a single S15 and then bead a **Peyote Stitch Decrease** in the next space*. Repeat from * to * five more times and then Step-Up to exit the first S15 added in this step (6 x S15).

STEP 12 - BLACK IN THE DIAGRAM

Using Peyote Stitch add 1 x S15 between each S15 added in the last step (6 x S15).

STEP 13 -GREEN IN THE DIAGRAM

*Using Peyote Stitch add a single S15 and then bead a **Peyote Stitch Decrease** in the next space*. Repeat from * to * twice more and then Step-Up to exit the first S15 added in this step. Lastly weave through all 3 x S15s added in this step to unite them and finish (3 x S15).

STEP 14

Add a **Hanging Loop** at the back of your bezel as desired.

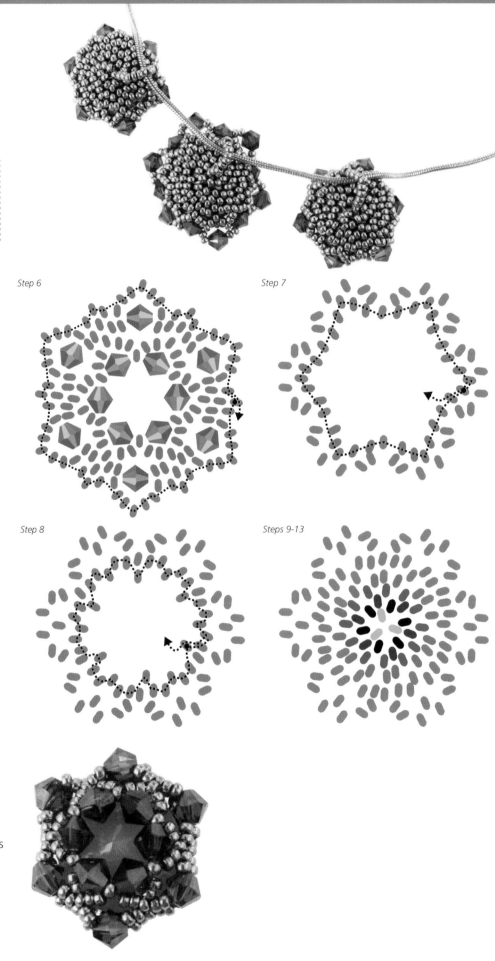

Step 6

Step 7

Step 8

Steps 9-13

ELABORATE BICONE BEZELS

Bead Steps 1-14 of the **Basic Bicone Bezel** then weave to exit any B added in Step 3. *Pick up 2 x S15s, 1B and 2 x S15s and then thread into the next B*. Repeat from * to * five more times to finish (24 x S15 and 6 x B).

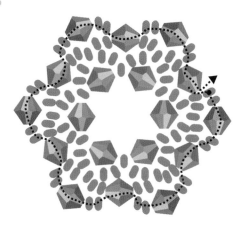

SIMPLER BICONE BEZELS

Bead Steps 1-14 of the **Basic Bicone Bezel** BUT at Step 3 pick up 7 x S15s and from then on treat the central 3 x S15s as your Bicone e.g. when Stepping-Up at the end of Step 3 you'll exit the 5th S15 in your loop of 7

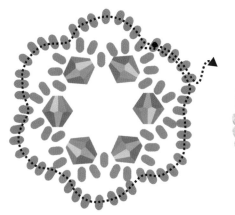

VARIATIONS

- Look at the **RAW Pearls Bezel variations** and **Super Crystal Petals** to see how you can add loops and then picots around your Bicones added in Step 3 or at the end of the Elaborate version

- You can bead into the back of your bail to add **Hanging Tabs** or tabs to join different bezels as shown on **Star Flowers**

- You can also add loops of 7 x S15s instead of the extra beads in the Elaborate version and then weave through again (missing out the central S15 in each loop to make it 'pop' out)

- In the **Elaborate** variation you can instead pick up 1 x S15, 1 Bicone and 1 x S15 for a different look as shown here

Crystal Coronas
Surround your Rivolis with extra sparkle

Materials

Each Basic Crystal Corona uses:
- 1 x 14mm Rivoli
- 2g of size 15 Miyuki seed beads - S15s
- 1g of size 11 cylinder beads - C beads
- 18 x 3mm bicones - B3 beads
- Finding of choice

Each Elaborate Corona uses:
- 1 x 14mm Rivoli
- 2g of size 15 Miyuki seed beads - S15s
- 1g of size 11 cylinder beads - C beads
- 36 x 3mm bicones - B3 beads
- 18 x 4mm bicones - B4 beads
- Finding of choice

I used
- Rivoli: Yellow Opal
- Seed beads: Miyuki #4202
- Cylinder beads: DB1763
- Bicones: Jet x 2AB

Techniques
- Stitch-In-The-Ditch, Page 11
- Basic Bezelling Technique, Page 12

BASIC CRYSTAL CORONA
STEP 1
Using the **Basic Bezelling Technique** bezel your Rivoli.

STEP 2
Weave to exit a C bead in the central round and using **SITD**, and 5 x S15 for each stitch, add 18 loops around your Bezel. Step-Up at the end to exit the 3rd S15 added (90 x S15).

STEP 3
Repeat Step 2 to add another round of 5 x S15 loops this time threading into the 3rd S15 of the loops added in the previous step (90 x S15).

> **TOP TIP**
> *I recommend beading at the front of your bezels when adding the bicones to ensure they sit nicely on top of your seed beads*

> **TOP TIP**
> *I used Basic Coronas for my earrings with findings simply stitched on, and an Elaborate Corona for a pendant with a* **Hanging Loop** *(Page 19) added to the back*

STEP 4
Repeat Step 3 to add another round of 5 x S15 loops but at the end don't Step-Up, instead stay exiting the 3rd S15 added in a loop in the previous step (90 x S15).

STEP 5
Weave from 'loop point' to 'loop point' threading through beads added in Step 3 to add 1 x B3 into each space. Then add a Hanging Loop at the back or earring finding as desired (18 x B3).

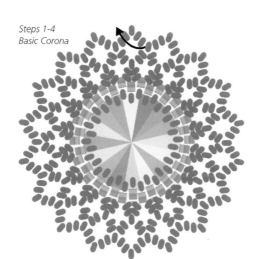

*Steps 1-4
Basic Corona*

Step 5 - Basic Corona

ELABORATE CORONA
STEP 1
Bead Steps 1-5 of the **Basic Crystal Corona** Bezel and then Step-Up to exit the 3rd S15 in one of the loops added in Step 4.

STEP 2
Repeat the principle of Steps 4-5 but adding 8 x S15s in each loop (144 x S15 and 18 x B3).

STEP 3
Step-Up to exit the 4th S15 in any of the 8-bead loops. *Pick up 1 x S15 and thread into the 5th S15 in the loop. Pick up 1 x B4 and thread into the 4th S15 in the next Loop*. Repeat from * to * seventeen more times then add a Hanging Loop or earring finding as desired (18 x S15, 18 x B4).

> **TOP TIP**
> *The loops of S15s on your bezels will be 'wobbly' and not laying in nice loops until you add your bicones so don't worry about this*

Steps 1-2 - Elaborate Corona

Step 3 - Elaborate Corona

Shaped Beads

Get adventurous by venturing
into adding different shapes &
styles of beads to your Rivolis...

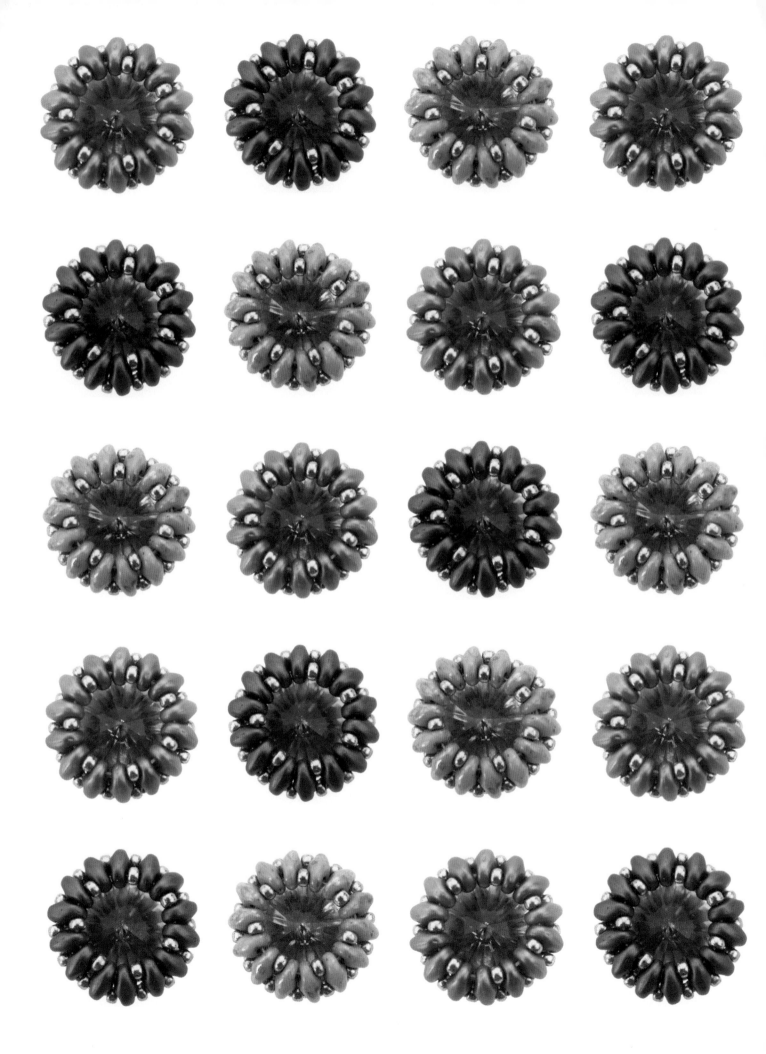

Super Dots
Use shaped beads to create quick & colourful bezels

These bezels are quick to bead and you can play around with colour in both the SuperDuos and the Rivolis.

Materials

Each Super Dot uses:
- 1 x 14mm Rivoli
- 1g of size 15 Miyuki seed beads - your S15 beads
- 1g of size 11 Miyuki seed beads - your S11 beads
- 14 x SuperDuo beads

I used
- Rivoli: Light Peach
- Seed beads: #4203
- SuperDuos: #43400, #94105 and #25043

THE STEPS...

STEP 1
Round One.
On a comfortable length of thread pick up 1 x S11 and 2 x SD. Repeat 6 more times and then thread through the first S11 to join into a circle. Weave through the full circle of beads a few times to hold them tight, finishing by exiting an SD and then using your preferred method (see below) to Step-Up into an empty hole in any SD (7 x S11, 14 x SD).

STEP 2
Round Two.
Pick up 1 x S11 and thread into the next SD. Repeat 13 more times to fill in the whole circle and finish exiting an S11 (14 x S11).

STEP 3
Adding Fringes.
Pick up 6 x S15 and, missing the last one, thread back through 4. Pick up 1 x S15 and thread into the next S11 added in the last step. Repeat from * to * 13 more times to add 14 Fringes and then Step-Up to exit the 6th S15 added in any Fringe – this is a Fringe End Bead (98 x S15).

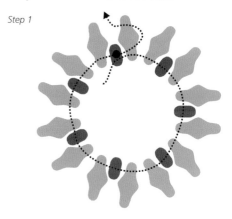

Step 1

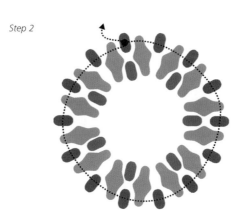

Step 2

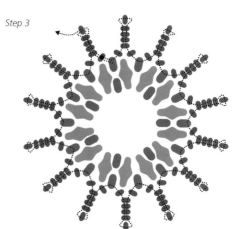

Step 3

Stepping-Up with SuperDuos

There are 2 methods you can use to Step-Up to exit the other hole in your SuperDuos:

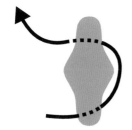

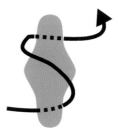

The first method is to simply thread into the other hole but this will result in you changing direction and your thread may show on the side of the bead

The other method is to thread behind the SD and into the other hole of the bead working in the same direction.
If you make sure the thread sits at the back of your bead it won't show and you'll carry on working in the same direction. This method can be fiddlier to bead, depending on what you're making

STEP 4

Loosely weave through all the Fringe End beads until you have joined all 14 of them. Lay your Rivoli so it faces out of the beads added in Step 1 and then pull your thread tight to bring the fringes together at the back. Weave around and around the Fringe End beads to pull tight and then weave away your threads to finish.

Step 4

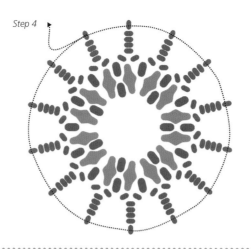

Hanging Loops

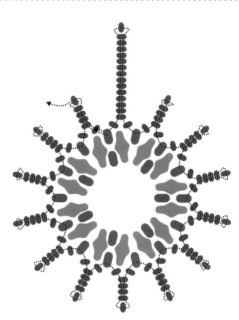

Adding a Hanging Loop at the edge:
Weave to exit any S11 added in Step 2. Pick up as many S15 beads as needed (threading into an earring finding if appropriate) and circle through the S11 you were exiting

Adding a larger Hanging Loop at the back:
For one of your fringes you can pick up more than 6 beads (e.g. 15) and then thread back down the extra beads to make a longer fringe. This will give you a larger loop at the back to thread a thicker stringing material behind

Covering the back of the Rivoli automatically gives you loops of seed beads which you can thread your chain or hanging material behind

Variations

Joining Bezels

Super Dots can be joined to each other to make bracelets.

You can do this by simply weaving to exit any S11 from Step 2, picking up as many S11 beads as desired and circling through an S11 on another bezel before picking up more S11 beads and circling back into the S11 you were exiting

Joining bezels using S11 beads which aren't directly opposite each other will let you make different shapes, for example a V-Shape which can be used as the centrepiece of a necklace

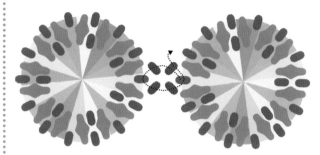

Adding extra decoration

You can add extra decoration around the edge of your bezel in a few different ways:

Adding Fringes:
Replicate what you beaded in Step 3 but only picking up 3 beads at the start. Then thread back through just 1 before picking up the last 1

Adding Picots:
Replicate what you did in Step 3 but just pick up loops with an uneven number of beads. Then weave around a second time missing out the central bead in each loop to make it pop out and become a Picot

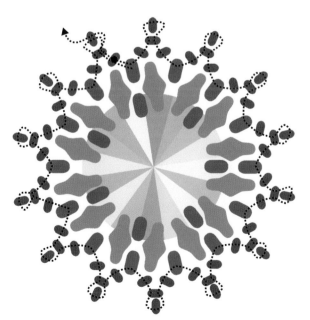

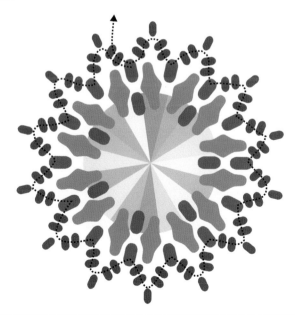

Super Flowers

Shaped beads give you a bezel with a floral theme and a reversible option

Working from the Basic Rivoli bezel and adding shaped beads embellishment gives you lots of design options…

Materials

Each Super Flower uses:
- 1 x 14mm Rivoli
- 1g of size 15 Miyuki seed beads - your S15 beads
- 1g of size 11 Cylinder beads - your C beads
- 18 x SuperDuo beads

Each Reversible Super Flower uses:
- 2 x 14mm Rivolis
- 1g of size 15 Miyuki seed beads - your S15 beads
- 2g of size 11 Cylinder beads - your C beads
- 54 x SuperDuo beads

I used
- Rivoli: Padparadscha, Rose Gold and Tanzanite
- Seed beads: #4203
- Cylinder beads: #262
- SuperDuos: #43400 and #24205

Techniques
- Stitch-In-The-Ditch, Page 11
- Basic Bezelling Technique, Page 12
- Stepping-Up with SuperDuos, Page 147
- Peyote Stitch

SUPER FLOWER

THE STEPS…

STEP 1
Flower Base.
Using the **Basic Bezelling Technique** bezel your Rivoli. Then, using **Stitch-In-The-Ditch**, add S15 beads on top of your central round of cylinder beads.

STEP 2
Adding the SuperDuos.
Add 1 x SD between each S15 added using **Stitch-In-The-Ditch.** Once you've added 18 Step-Up to exit the second hole in one of them (18 x SD).

STEP 3
Beginning the Picots.
Pick up 3 x S15 and thread into the empty hole in the next SD. Repeat 17 more times to fill in the whole circle and finish exiting the first S15 added (54 x S15).

STEP 4
Finishing the Picots.
Missing the second S15 in a group of 3, thread into the third, the next SD and then the first S15 in the next group of 3. Repeat this all around the circle so each central S15 ends up sticking out. At the end, weave to exit the bottom hole of any SD.

STEP 5
Weave between your SDs adding 1 x S15 in each space (18 x S15).

Step 1

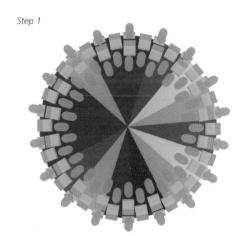

Step 2

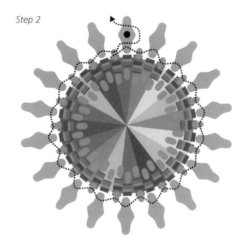

Step 3

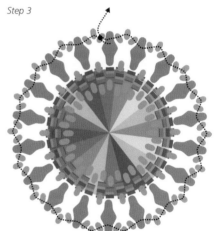

Step 4

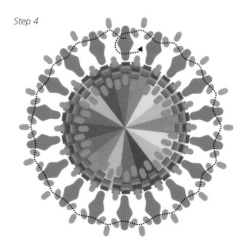

Step 5

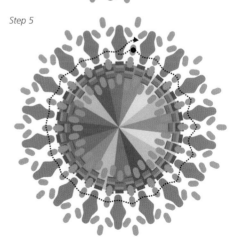

STEP 6
Hanging Loop.
At the back of your bezel weave to exit any S15 in the second round of S15s from the end. Pick up as many S15s as desired in your loop and then thread into the opposite S15 of the same round. Thread back through the new beads and circle into the S15 you were exiting.

REVERSIBLE SUPER FLOWER

THE STEPS...
STEP 1
Bead Steps 1-2 of a **Super Flower** and then add 1 x SD between each one already added. At the end Step-Up to exit the other hole of any SD.

STEP 2
Repeat the previous Step to add 1 more round of 18 x SD. As you do this you need to pull tight so that your work 'cups up' towards the back of your Rivoli (18 x SD).

> **TOP TIP**
> *If you want to add a fine chain to your Reversible Super Flower then, as you bead Step 3, you can thread it into place. This makes it easier to attach a chain rather than adding it later*

STEP 3
Repeat Step 1 of a **Super Flower** to bezel another Rivoli and then bring the two bezels together and replicate Step 2 of a **Super Flower** to zip the 2 Rivolis together making sure they sit back to back.

STEP 4
Repeat Step 5 of a **Super Flower** to add S15s at the front of each bezel (36 x S15).

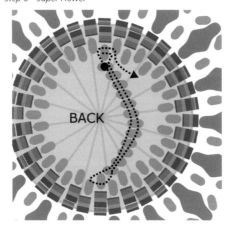

Step 6 - Super Flower

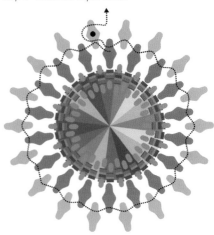

Step 1 - Reversible Super Flower

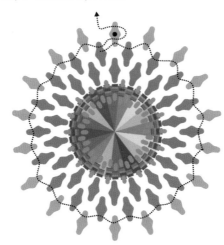

Step 2 - Reversible Super Flower

Step 4 - Reversible Super Flower

If you want to wear a Reversible Super Flower on a chain you'll find it easier if you add the chain before you finish Step 3

Variations

Adding a Hanging Loop at the edge

If you'd rather add a hanging loop to your **Reversible Super Flower**, then simply weave to exit a hole in the central round of SDs, pick up as many S15s as you'd like and thread into either the same SD or another one in the same round

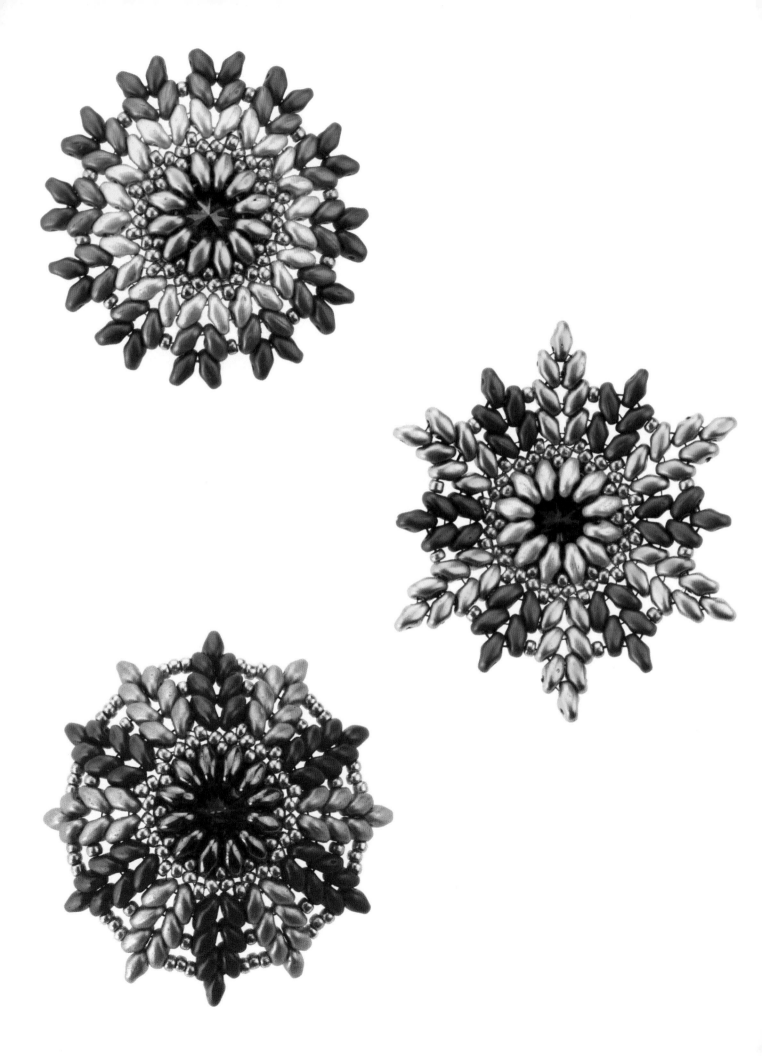

Wheat Sheaves

Materials

Each Wheat Sheaf uses:
- 1 x 14mm Rivoli
- 1g of size 15 Miyuki seed beads - S15
- 1g of size 11 Miyuki seed beads - S11
- 84 x SuperDuo beads

I used
- Rivoli: Peony Pink
- Seed beads: #4203
- SuperDuos: #24205, #25026, #94105, and #25043

Techniques
- Peyote Stitch Decrease, Page 11
- Stepping-Up with SuperDuos, Page 147
- Peyote Stitch

THE STEPS...

STEP 1
First Round of SuperDuos
Pick up 1 x S11 and 1 x SD. Repeat 11 more times until you've picked up 12 of each and then thread through the first S11 and SD to join into a circle.
Step-Up to exit the other hole in any SD and then thread through all the empty holes in your SDs to join them into a circle. Gently ease them so that the circle of beads lays flat and the S11s are outside the circle. Lastly, Step-Up to exit any S11 (12 x S11, 12 x SD).

STEP 2
Adding Picots.
Pick up 3 x S11 and thread into the next S11 added in the previous step. Repeat 11 more times to add 12 Picots. Then, at the end, Step-Up to exit the second S11 in a group of 3 (36 x S11).

STEP 3
Second Round of SuperDuos.
Pick up 2 x SD and thread into the second/central S11 in the next group of 3 x S11. Repeat 11 more times to add 24 x SD then Step-Up to exit the other hole in any SD bead facing towards the other SD in the pair (24 x SD).

STEP 4
Third Round of SuperDuos.
Pick up 2 x SD and thread into the empty hole in the other SD in the pair and then thread into the empty hole in the first SD in the next pair. Repeat 11 more times to add 24 x SD. Step-Up at the end to exit the empty hole in an SD facing towards the other SD in the pair (24 x SD).

STEP 5
Fourth Round of SuperDuos.
Pick up 2 x SD and thread into the empty hole in the other SD in the pair. Then pick up 1 x S11 and thread into the empty hole in the next first SD in a pair. Repeat 11 more times to add 24 x SD (24 x SD and 12 x S11).

STEP 6
Covering the Back – Round One.
Weave to exit any S11s added in Step 1. Pick up 5 x S15 and thread into the next S11 added in Step 1. Repeat 11 more times to add 12 x 5-bead loops and then Step-Up to exit the 3rd bead in the first loop (60 x S15).

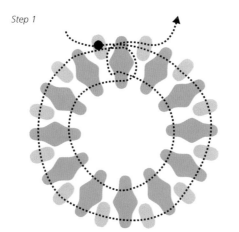

Step 1

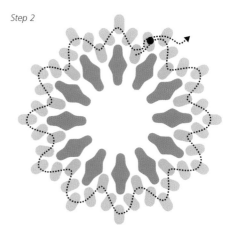

Step 2

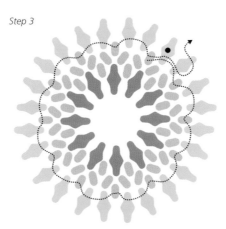

Step 3

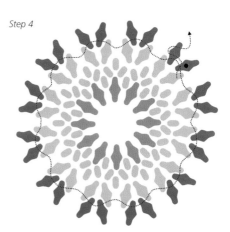

Step 4

Step 5

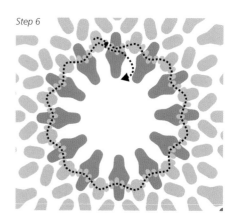

Step 6

Main photo from top: As instructions, 'Different heights' variation, 'Adding a Point Round' variation

STEP 7
Covering the Back – Round Two.
Insert your Rivoli so it faces out of the beadwork added in Steps 1-4.
Pick up 3 x S15 and thread into the 3rd bead in the next loop added in the last round. Repeat from * to * 11 more times and Step-Up to exit the 2nd bead added in the 1st loop in this step (36 x S15).

STEP 8
Covering the Back – Round Three.
Add a round with loops of 2 x S15s, threading into the 2nd S15 in each loop from the last round.
At the end of the round, Step-Up to exit the 1st bead added in the 1st loop (24 x S15).

STEP 9
Covering the Back – Round Four.
Using Peyote Stitch, add 1 x S15 and thread into the 1st bead in the next loop added in the last round. Repeat eleven more times and at the end of the round Step-Up to exit the first bead added (12 x S15).

STEP 10
Covering the Back – Round Five.
Using Peyote Stitch, add 1 x S15 between each one added in the last round (12 x S15).

STEP 11
Covering the Back – Round Six.
Using Peyote Stitch, add 1 x S15 and then, using a **Peyote Stitch Decrease**, decrease the next space. Repeat this pattern 5 more times and finish the round by Stepping-Up to exit the first bead added (6 x S15).

STEP 12
Covering the Back – Round Seven.
Using Peyote Stitch add 1 x S15 into each space from the last round (6 x S15).

STEP 13
Covering the Back – Round Eight.
Using Peyote Stitch, add 1 x S15 and then, using a **Peyote Stitch Decrease**, decrease the next space. Repeat this pattern 2 more times and finish the round by Stepping-Up to exit the first bead added. Weave around these 3 beads to secure and finish (3 x S15).

Step 7
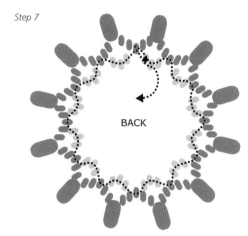

Step 8
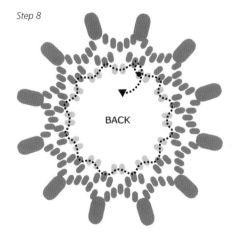

Step 9
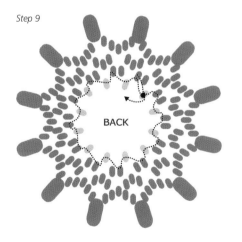

Step 10
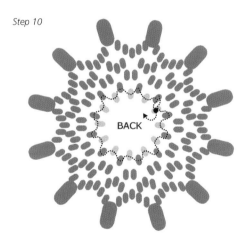

Step 11
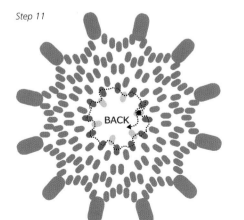

Step 12
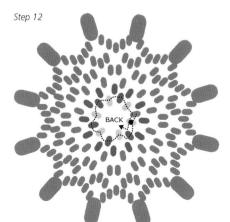

Step 13
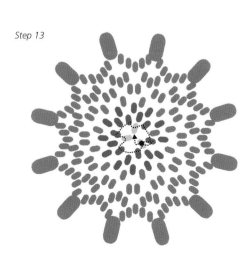

Variations

Adding a Point Round

If you want to add Points on the top of each SD group, then add another round similar to Step 5 (Fourth Round of SuperDuos) but adding 1 x SD on top of each pair added in the last round and, as you thread between groups of SD beads, pick up as many S11 or S15 beads as needed to keep your work flat.

You can also add the 'Point Round' at any time after Step 3 or 4 (with or without extra seed beads as needed) for smaller versions.

You can also have the SD sections be different heights.
You can bead this by adding, in the third round of SD beads, just 1 on top of alternate stacks and 2 on the others.
Then, when you add the fourth round, add single ones on top of the taller stacks and nothing on the others

As you do this you'll need to weave from one hole to the other in some SDs (using your preferred method) to get to the position to add new beads and move through your work. You can see where you need to do that with the solid lines in the diagram below:

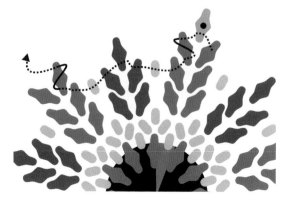

Super Crystal Petals
Unite different bead shapes for a sparkling ornate bezel

Materials
Each Super Crystal Petal uses:
- 1 x 14mm Rivoli
- 2g of size 15 Miyuki seed beads - S15
- 27 x 4mm bicones
- 18 x SuperDuo beads

Each Extra Sparkling Crystal Petal uses:
- 1 x 14mm Rivoli
- 2g of size 15 Miyuki seed beads - S15
- 36 x 4mm bicones
- 18 x SuperDuo beads

Each Extra Super Crystal Petal uses:
- 1 x 14mm Rivoli
- 2g of size 15 Miyuki seed beads - S15
- 27 x 4mm bicones
- 45 x SuperDuo beads

I used
- Rivoli: Topaz & Crystal Dark Red
- Seed beads: #4203
- Bicones: Siam & Arum x 2
- SuperDuos: #01890 and #01780

Techniques
- Stepping-Up with SuperDuos, Page 147
- Wheat Sheaves, Page 154
- Peyote Stitch

THE STEPS...
STEP 1
First Round.
Pick up 1 x S15 and 1 x Bicone. Repeat 8 more times until you've picked up 9 of each and then thread through the first S15 to join into a circle.
Weave around the circle a few times to pull tight and then finish by exiting an S15 (9 x S15, 9 x Bicones).

STEP 2
Adding Loops.
Pick up 5 x S15 and thread into the next S15 added in the previous step. Repeat 8 more times to add 9 Loops and then at the end Step-Up to exit the third S15 in a group of 5 (45 x S15).

STEP 3
Second Round of Bicones.
Pick up 1 x S15, 1 Bicone and 1 x S15. Thread into the third S15 in the next Loop added in the last round. Repeat 8 more times to add 9 groups of beads. Finish by Stepping-Up to exit a Bicone (18 x S15s and 9 x Bicones).

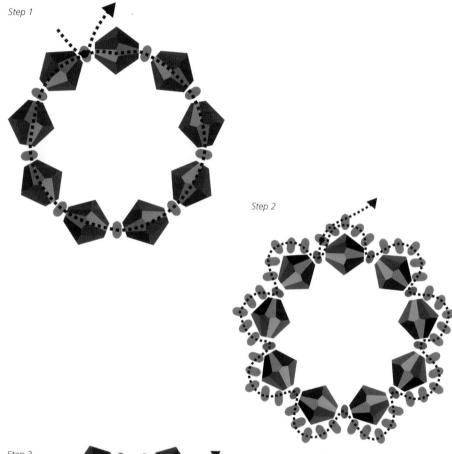

Step 1

Step 2

Step 3

Main photo from top: Super Crystal Petal, Extra Sparkling Crystal Petal, Extra Super Crystal Petal

STEP 4

Adding SuperDuos.
Pick up 1 x SD, 1 x S15 and 1 x SD.
Thread into the next Bicone. Repeat 8
more times. Finish by Stepping-Up to exit
the empty hole in the first SD in a pair
facing towards the other SD in the pair
(18 x SD and 9 x S15).

STEP 5

Third Round of Bicones.
*Pick up 1 x S15, 1 Bicone and 1 x S15.
Thread into the other SD in the pair and
then pick up 1 x S15 and thread in the
first SD in the next pair*. Repeat from *
to * 8 more times to complete the round,
finishing by Stepping-Up to exit the first
S15 before a Bicone (9 x Bicones and 27
x S15).

STEP 6

Beginning Picots.
*Pick up 6 x S15 and thread into the S15
on the other side of the Bicone. Thread
through 1 x SD, 1 x S15, 1 x SD and 1
x S15 to exit the S15 before the next
Bicone*. Repeat from * to * eight more
times and then finish by Stepping-Up to
exit the 3rd S15 added in a Loop (54 x
S15).

Step 4

Step 5

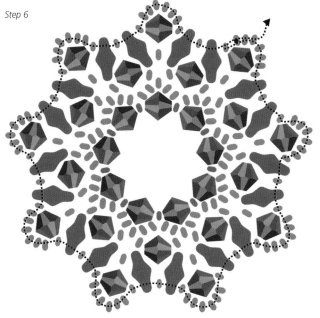

Step 6

Step 7

Step 8

STEP 7
Finishing Picots.
Pick up 1 x S15 and thread through the next 3 x S15s in the Loop and then 1 x S15, 1 x SD, 1 x S15, 1 x SD and 4 x S15s to exit the 3rd S15 in the next Loop. Repeat from * to * eight more times to finish the round (9 x S15).

STEP 8
Beginning the Back.
Weave to exit an S15 added in Step 3 that was picked up after a Bicone facing towards another Bicone.
Pick up 1 x S15 and thread into the next S15 from Step 3 which sits before a Bicone. Pick up 5 x S15s and thread into the next S15 which sits after a Bicone.
Repeat from * to * eight more times to complete the round and Step-Up to exit the 3rd bead added in a Loop (54 x S15).

STEP 9
Finishing the back.
You now need to bead the principle of Steps 7-12 of '**Wheat Sheaves**' to finish the back BUT as you have a different number of sections (and an odd-number of them) at Step 11 you'll bead 4 repeats and then add a single bead.
Then at Step 12 you'll add 5 beads and then weave around them to finish.

EXTRA SPARKLING CRYSTAL PETALS

This variation has an extra round of Bicones and their surrounding Loops & Picots

STEP 1

Bead Steps 1-7 of **Super Crystal Petals** and then Step-Up to exit the seventh S15 in the any of the Picot Loops (it will be the 6th S15 in any loop added in Step 6).

STEP 2

Pick up 1 x S15, 1 Bicone and 1 x S15. Thread into the first S15 in the next Picot Loop and thread through all the beads in the Loop to exit the seventh one. Repeat to add a total of 9 new groups of beads and Step-Up at the end to exit the first S15 added in a group (9 x Bicones, 18 x S15).

STEP 3

Repeat the principle of Steps 6-7 of **Super Crystal Petals** to add Loops and then Picots around the new Bicones. As you add the Loops you'll weave through all 7 x S15 beads in the previous Loops & Picots.

STEP 4

Bead Steps 8-9 of **Super Crystal Petals** to cover the back of your piece.

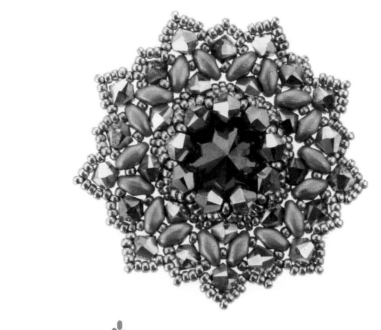

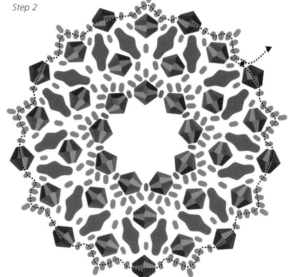

Step 2

Step 3

EXTRA SUPER CRYSTAL PETALS

This variation has extra rounds of SuperDuo beads

STEP 1
Bead Steps 1-4 of **Super Crystal Petals.**
Next replicate Step 5 but using 1 x SD, 1
x S15 and 1 x SD (instead of S15, Bicone
and S15) inbetween the SDs in a pair and
then 1 x S15 inbetween pairs of SDs.
Step-Up at the end of the round to exit
the empty hole of the first SD in a pair
facing towards the other one in the pair
(18 x SD, 18 x S15).

STEP 2
Add a round with 1 x SD inbetween the
SD bead pairs from the last round and 1
x S15, 1 Bicone and 1 x S15 between the
pairs of SDs from the last round (9 x SD,
18 x S15 and 9 x Bicones).

STEP 3
Repeat the principle of Steps 6-7 of **Super
Crystal Petals** to add Loops and then
Picots around the new Bicones.
As you add the Loops you'll weave
through a S15, 3 x SDs and an S15 (63 x
S15).

STEP 4
Bead Steps 8-9 of **Super Crystal Petals** to
cover the back of your piece.

Step 1

Step 2

Step 3

Claw Bezels
Grab a hold of your Rivoli with these striking beads

Materials
Each Claw Bezel uses:
- 1 x 14mm Rivoli
- 1g of size 15 Miyuki seed beads - S15
- 1g of size 11 Miyuki seed beads - S11
- 12 x 3x10mm Crescent beads - CR
- Findings of choice - I used earring findings and small tassels but these are optional

I used
- Rivoli: Majestic Blue
- Seed beads: #4202
- Crescents: Matte Gold Metallic

Techniques
- Peyote Stitch Decrease, Page 11
- Stepping-Up with SuperDuos, Page 147
- Peyote Stitch

THE STEPS...
STEP 1
Base Ring.
Pick up 1 x S11 and 1 x CR. Repeat from * to * eleven more times until you have 12 of each. Circle through the first S11 to join into a ring and then all around the beads again finishing by exiting an S11 (12 x S11 and 12 x CR).

STEP 2
Beading the back.
Pick up 3 x S15 and thread into the next S11. Repeat 11 more times and then Step-Up to exit the 2nd S15 (36 x S15).

STEP 3
Pick up 3 x S15 and thread into the 2nd S15 in the next 3-bead loop added in the last round. Repeat 11 more times and then Step-Up to exit the 2nd S15 (36 x S15).

STEP 4
Repeat Step 3.

STEP 5
Pick up 1 x S15 and thread into the 2nd S15 in the next 3-bead loop added in the last round. Repeat 11 more times and then Step-Up to exit the first S15 (12 x S15).

STEP 6
Insert your Rivoli and then bead a round of Peyote Stitch with 1 x S15 between each from the previous step (12 x S15).

STEP 7
*Using Peyote Stitch add 1 x S15 into each of the next 2 spaces and then bead a **Peyote Stitch Decrease** in the next*. Repeat from * to * three more times (8 x S15).

STEP 8
Bead a round of Peyote Stitch with 1 x S15 between each bead of the previous step including just 1 in each large space made by the decreasing (8 x S15).

STEP 9
*Using Peyote Stitch add 1 x S15 into a space and then bead a **Peyote Stitch Decrease** in the next*. Repeat from * to * three more times (4 x S15).

STEP 10
Bead a round of Peyote Stitch with 1 x S15 between each from the previous step including just 1 in each large space made by the decreasing. Then weave through all 4 new beads to unite them (4 x S15).

STEP 11
Weave through your work and then Step-Up to exit the empty hole in any Crescent, just as you would with a SuperDuo (described on Page 147).

STEP 12
Pick up 5 x S15 and thread into the next Crescent. Repeat all around to add loops between each Crescent and then Step-Up to exit the 2nd bead in the first loop (60 x S15).

STEP 13
Adding Picots - Optional.
Missing the 3rd S15 (this will make it 'pop out') thread through the 4th and 5th S15, the Crescent and then the 1st and 2nd S15 in the next loop. Repeat from * to * eleven more times to finish the round (no beads),

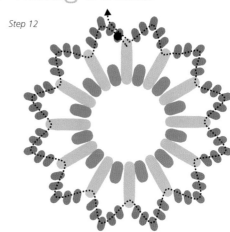

Step 12

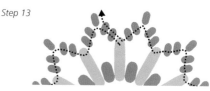

Step 13

> **TOP TIP**
> If you want to add findings or tassels etc. then pick them up in the appropriate spot when adding loops of S15 beads in Step 12

> **TOP TIP**
> After Step 1 you'll be working at the back of your bezel so make sure to have the Crescent beads facing you with their 'claws' up

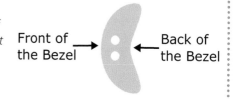

Front of the Bezel → ← Back of the Bezel

My final word...

...Experiment!

All the bezels and projects in this book can be experimented with, whether that's changing the Rivoli size, altering colours, swapping pearls for crystals, turning an earring into a pendant, changing the shaped bead you use and many, many more options.

Persevere and, even if the project doesn't have the exact effect you were planning on, you'll soon have some sparkly, unique beadwork to call your own

For example, these pendants began with me taking a Rivoli bezelled using the **Basic Bezelling Technique** and then adding (using **Stitch-In-The-Ditch** - see Page 11) SuperDuos with picots made from 5 x S15s...

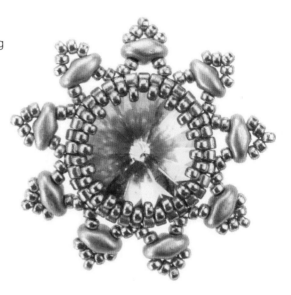

...Then I swapped the SuperDuos for Bricks and the Picots for smaller strands of S15s...

...Next I swapped the Bricks for Gem Duos and the Picots for simple loops...

...I'll show you what I did next in Volume 2...

This book is dedicated to all the beaders, beading venues and bead shops all around the world who support and encourage me through purchasing my work, attending classes with me, stocking my products, asking me to teach for you and showing me photos of what you've made from my instructions.

You motivate me to create new, original and hopefully inspiring beadwork and so this book is for you

Printed in Great
Britain
by Amazon